# The Local Management of Schools
## A Handbook for Teachers, Governors and Parents

**Resources in Education**

Other titles in this series:

*The School Library: Responding to Change*, Elizabeth King MA ALA
*The School Meals Service*, Nan Berger OBE FHCIMA

**Resources in Education**

# The Local Management of Schools

Brent Davies & Chris Braund

Northcote House

Davies, Brent
    Local management of schools: an introduction for teachers,
    governors and parents. —
    (Resources in education)
    1. England. Schools. Management — Case studies
    I. Title II. Braund, Chris III. Series
    371.2′00942

    ISBN 0-7463-0574-5     371.2

    CEN       12 FEB 1990

© 1989 by Brent Davies & Chris Braund

First published in 1989 by Northcote House Publishers Ltd, Harper & Row House, Estover Road, Plymouth PL6 7PZ, United Kingdom. Tel: Plymouth (0752) 705251. Fax: (0752) 777603. Telex: 45635.

All rights reserved. No part of this work may be reproduced or stored in an information retrieval system (other than short extracts for the purposes of review) without the express permission of the Publishers given in writing.

Typeset by PDQ Typesetting, Stoke-on-Trent.

Printed in Great Britain by BPCC Wheatons Ltd, Exeter

# Contents

|  | Preface | 7 |
|---|---|---|
| 1 | What is Local Management of Schools (LMS)? | 11 |
| 2 | Experience of LEA Schemes to Date | 22 |
| 3 | School Costs and School Budgets | 29 |
| 4 | Managing the School Budget | 39 |
| 5 | Headteachers and the Management of LMS | 47 |
| 6 | Implications for Governors, LEAs and the School Community | 55 |
| 7 | Developing School Management Plans | 67 |
| 8 | Management Action Points | 73 |
| 9 | Management Exercises and Case Studies | 75 |
|  | Appendix 1: The School Budget in 1992 – What a Governors' Report Might Look Like | 80 |
|  | Appendix 2: Obtaining Grant Maintained Status – Opting Out | 87 |
|  | Glossary | 91 |
|  | Further Reading | 93 |
|  | Useful Addresses | 94 |
|  | Index | 95 |

# Preface

This book has been written to provide a simple and clear explanation of Local Management of Schools (LMS). Rather than trying to provide another technical manual in this field, we have sought to provide an introduction that the non-specialist in educational finance can understand. The book is designed to highlight the key elements and stages in understanding and operating delegated school budgets. It avoids jargon and is written to offer the reader with little knowledge of the subject a clear understanding of this new and important area of school management.

The book is meant for Headteachers with limited or no experience of delegated school finance, and for school staff who want to understand the nature of this change. It should be essential reading, too, for new school governors who want to understand the new framework of delegated budgets and their responsibilities in managing these budgets in co-operation with the Head in a school. Local Authority advisers and officers will also find it an invaluable introduction to the changing nature of school finance.

Local Management of Schools brings a fundamental change in the way schools are financed, organised and operate. It is likely to prove one of the most significant changes in our education system. It represents a revolutionary change in the relationship between central government, Local Education Authorities (LEAs), the schools and the communities which they serve.

Since 1945 central government has traditionally provided financial support for education in the form of grants to supplement money raised locally through rates. The Local Education Authority received both these sums, and was responsible for spending them on the schools. The LEA decided how many staff a school had, how much was spent on books and equipment, how much was spent on maintenance, decoration and heating. The school was responsible for delivering the curriculum within resources provided by the LEA. It could not move money from one expenditure area to another if it thought that was a better way to spend it. It also had no incentive to economise, as any savings were retained by the LEA and not by the school. In short, the LEA retained the power over all expenditure decisions, with the school responsible for delivering the curriculum.

However, in LMS this power is shifted from the LEA to the individual school level. Schools will now be given a total budget figure but, acting within that total, can allocate the budget between staffing and other resources as they see fit. For example schools will now determine the number of teachers, bearing in mind other expenditure needs. Thus, the LEA's control over the appropriate mix of resources will disappear. However, by gaining this responsibility, schools will also gain accountability. They can no longer blame the LEA. The governors, in consultation with the Headteacher and staff, will be accountable to the parents for the school and how its resources are deployed. A typical primary school of 200 pupils prior to this change had control of £3,000 for books and learning materials. Now with LMS it will be responsible for a budget in excess of £250,000. A secondary school of 1400 pupils could have a budget of £1,750,000!

How has this radical change come about? Early experiments in devolving financial responsibility were pioneered by such authorities as the ILEA, Cheshire and Cambridgeshire. They developed the idea that the nearer to the teaching operation decisions were taken the more appropriate those decisions would be. Thus some experience was being gained about increased efficiency in schools which took their own decisions.

This idea of **delegated finance** was picked up by the Conservative Government and embodied in the 1988 Education Act. Clearly, the resources which a school receives are determined largely by the number of pupils on its school roll. The more pupils it attracts, the more money it receives; it can then decide how to spend that money. A policy of **open enrolments**, in which parents can choose which school their children attend, tends to reinforce this process. If schools provide education of a kind the parents want then they will attract more pupils and hence more money, enabling them to take on extra staff, etc. However, they become painfully accountable if they do not provide the education which the parents want. If the parents take the children away, the school loses money and has to decide how to reduce expenditure.

In this book we will examine the details of LMS and the management issues involved. We will then discuss the financial details which governors, teachers and other interested parties need to understand. The development of appropriate **management plans** to run this new system are outlined to form a basis upon which schools can then act. No one can predict what the full effect of these changes will be but one thing is certain—the nature of schools and school management will be very different in future. This book is meant for those coming to terms with these changes.

We would like to acknowledge the help of David Henderson who gave us permission to reproduce his 'governors' report' for 1992. Brent Davies would like to thank Hazel, Cassandra and Rhiannon for their patience and support while writing this book. Chris Braund would similarly like to acknowledge the debt he owes to Diane, Rachael and Mark for their help during the genesis of this book.

# 1
# What is Local Management of Schools?

Local Management of Schools (LMS) comes under a number of confusing titles such as Local Financial Management, Delegated or Devolved Finance and Cost Centres. These all mean that most of the school expenditure previously allocated by the Local Education Authority will now be allocated by the school governors in consultation with the headteacher. Thus the LEA will determine the total amount of money a school will receive (its budget) but how this is spent—in terms of the number of teachers, the amount of furniture, the amount of heating and the amount of books and materials—will be left for the school to decide, as long as it keeps its spending within the overall budget limit. This therefore involves a change:

- **Present practice:** The LEA provides teachers, heating and lighting, maintenance, books and materials, examination fees, etc. The school gets fixed amounts of these resources as determined by the LEA.
- **Future practice:** The LEA provides a lump sum (the budget) and the school decides how much it wants, and can afford, of each resource; for example, more teachers OR more books and materials.

In this chapter we will look at a number of key factors which will explain the nature and dimensions of delegated school finance.

## WHY DELEGATE FINANCIAL CONTROL?

The central belief behind delegated finance in schools is that if the schools themselves can determine what resources to employ to meet the children's needs then they will make better choices than remote LEA officers. The Government has put forward the following central objectives for delegated finance:

1. To enable governing bodies and headteachers to direct resources to the needs and priorities of their schools as they see them.
2. To make schools more responsive to their clients—parents, pupils, employers and community.
3. Thereby to improve the quality of teaching and learning within the resources available.

## TO WHOM IS FINANCIAL CONTROL DELEGATED?

Financial control of the school's budget is delegated to the governors of the school. In practice, much of the detailed control over expenditure may be delegated by the governors to the head, but *it is the governors of the schools who have the final responsibility for the budget.*

This, together with the fact that the LEA is no longer responsible for appointing and dismissing staff (although it is responsible for paying them), means that governing bodies have significant new powers and responsibilities. On the staffing question the Education Reform Act gives the following responsibility to a governing body:

> "It will determine the number of both teaching and non-teaching staff at the school, will select for appointment and will be able to require dismissal, taking account of the professional advice of the Chief Education Officer, his staff and the Head teacher."

The role of governors has therefore become much more important—an issue which is discussed in Chapter Six.

## WHICH SCHOOLS ARE INVOLVED IN DELEGATION?

This is very simple:
1. All secondary schools.
2. All primary schools with 200 or more pupils.
3. Smaller primary schools elected (after consultation) by the LEA.
4. Special schools elected by the LEA (initially outside scheme).

Thus the LEA has to include schools in the first two categories but can choose whether to delegate finance to the governing bodies of its smaller primary schools and special schools.

## WHAT IS DELEGATED TO SCHOOLS?

In order to give an overview this can be taken as salaries of staff employed to work in the schools, day to day premises costs, books and equipment and other goods and services. It is worth remembering that only primary and secondary schools are covered by the scheme—it excludes youth, careers and adult education.

An easy way to think about delegation is as a landlord and tenant arrangement. The landlord (the LEA) is responsible for the major exterior building structure and repairs; the tenant (the school) is responsible for internal expenditure on teachers and internal heating and maintenance. Thus the school will have a lump sum budget from which it will decide how much to spend on different priorities. It doesn't receive the cash—the LEA retains that. The school only has the power to direct the expenditure. Typical areas it will now have control of are:

- Buildings – internal maintenance.
- Equipment – furniture and fittings;
  – specific educational equipment.
- Rent and rates.
- Fuel and light.
- Textbooks, library books, stationery, materials and equipment.
- Printing, office stationery, postage and telephone.
- Domestic and cleaning materials and equipment.
- Staff travelling, educational visits.
- Examination fees.
- Staffing – teachers, technicians, classroom assistants, secretarial and administration staff.

## WHAT IS RETAINED BY THE LEA?

First we need to understand the three stage budget classification used in delegated finance.

1. **General Schools Budget** – all direct and indirect costs of running schools incurred both at the schools and at the central LEA administration level.
2. **Aggregated Schools Budget** – that part of the general schools budget left for distribution to schools when **mandatory** and **discretionary** exceptions have been deducted by the LEA.

3. **Delegated Budget** – the amount apportioned to a school out of an aggregated school budget.

So LEAs do not pass on all financial control. They remain responsible for what the Act lays down as mandatory and discretionary exceptions. Only then are schools allocated what is left to spend on priorities as they see fit.

**Items of expenditure over which LEAs will be required to retain direct control (mandatory exceptions)**

Major capital expenditure, Central Government grants and LEA administration and advisory expenditure stay with the LEA and are not delegated to the schools. In detail these items are:

1. Capital expenditure and debt charges.
2. Expenditure which results from specific government grants for the LEA to fund:
   A. Education Support Grants for identified government initiatives.
   B. LEA training grants.
   C. Section 11 grants – extra help for English as a second language in certain schools.
   D. Travellers' children's grants.
   E. Technical and Vocational Educational Initiative (TVEI).
3. Items prescribed by regulations:
   A. Central administration (including internal audit, legal advice and related services).
   B. Inspectors/Advisers.
   C. Specific grants from the European Community.
   D. Home to school transport.

**Note:** Items 3A and 3B are subject to review by the Secretary of State. This is very important because schools may one day receive a financial allocation for advisory help which they can choose to spend either on LEA advisers or on other areas. This may have considerable effects on the quality of the advisory service and, perhaps, on the number of advisers.

**Discretionary exceptions**
These are items of expenditure and services over which LEAs may wish to retain direct control. This is an interesting category. The

## What is Local Management of Schools?

LEA can choose whether to delegate financial responsibility for a particular area to schools or retain it for itself. School meals are one such area, but they will shortly have to be put out to private tender. That leaves:

1. Certain specialised services, eg
   - structural repairs and maintenance
   - premises and equipment insurance
   - provision for statemented pupils and special units
   - child guidance and education welfare
   - peripatetic and advisory teachers
   - pupil support, uniforms etc.

2. LEA initiatives (eg for curriculum development)

3. Staff costs eg
   - special staff costs (eg safeguarding supply cover, public duty absences)
   - dismissals and premature retirements
   - insurance for governors

4. Contingency reserves eg
   - unforeseen cost increases
   - large unforeseen changes in pupil numbers
   - emergencies, eg fire damage
   - correction of errors

The limit that the LEA can spend on these discretionary categories once school meals, costs of premature retirement and severance and governors insurance have been taken out, should not exceed 10% of the LEA's general schools budget (GSB) for an initial period (max. three years) and 7% of the GSB thereafter. This is very important because with the high cost of these services it is unlikely that an LEA could retain control of all of them and stay within these limits. Thus some of the items and parts of others will have to be delegated to schools. This will significantly change the role of the LEA.

## HOW WILL FINANCE BE DELEGATED TO SCHOOLS?

Experience in the many pilot schemes to date has been based on **historical costing**. This means that the money which a school receives in its budget is largely determined by what it has received in previous years (its history). There are adjustments from year to year as pupil numbers and other factors fluctuate but the basic budget follows an historic pattern. The minor adjustment from year to year is called an **incremental** approach.

One of the key factors that emerged in the pilot schemes which is now apparent to all LEAs grappling with LMS is that it is not known how much a particular school costs to run. While an LEA knows the staffing cost for each school, the costs the school incurs in terms of grounds maintenance, support services, etc are not always clear. This is because these amounts are paid as a *total* by the LEA for all its schools: it has not in the past calculated how much each school has cost and apportioned that amount to it.

Thus the two areas that LEAs are working on at present are

- an accurate system of determining each school's precise costs;
- a method of distributing money to schools.

In determining the method of distribution the 1988 Act lays down that each LEA will have to work out its own formula for distributing funds and will not be able to use historical cost. While each LEA is free to devise its own formula, that formula must have the following features:

- It should be simple, clear and predictable in its impact.
- It should be determined by pupil numbers, age-weighted for at least 75% of its budget.
- The formula should allow for the extra costs of children with learning difficulties, and the extra costs of small schools.
- It should give incentives to schools to make the most effective use of their budgets by charging actual costs.

These factors, as will be shown in Chapter Three, will make a fundamental impact on schools. If three-quarters of a school's income is to be determined by pupil numbers then schools with high cost structures will be penalised compared with low cost schools. For example, two identical schools with 900 pupils each will receive the same amount of money for the pupil number part of the formula, ie 75%, but may have different cost structures. One school may have older staff with salaries at the top end of the incremental scale, the other younger staff nearer the bottom end. Both will receive the same amount of money but the first school may have an extra £30,000 to £40,000 on its salary bill. This is what is meant by charging actual costs. There will be some protection for schools with ten staff or less who may be severely affected by being

# What is Local Management of Schools?

charged actual salary costs. The Government will allow some transitional arrangements, lasting up to four years, by LEAs in order to ease the problem. However, a formula method will act to the benefit of some schools and the detriment of others. If money follows pupils, it could be said that we have a 'voucher scheme' by a different name.

## WHAT CONTROL WILL A SCHOOL HAVE OVER THE KEY RESOURCE OF STAFFING?

Staffing certainly involves one of the most radical changes in the relationship between LEAs and their schools. From 1st September 1988 governors are responsible for appointing, disciplining and dismissing staff, rather than the LEA. If this is put into the context of LMS (when it comes into operation) it can be seen that the governors of county schools will have the power to decide:

- The numbers and grades of a school's staff (as long as they are operating within the budget).
- All appointments.
- Disciplinary and grievance procedures.
- Suspensions.
- Dismissals.

The Education Reform Act (1988) states that the headteacher must be consulted and that the Chief Education Officer or his representative has the right to attend governors' meetings and give advice. It can be seen, however, that a very significant shift of power has taken place which greatly enhances governors' control over staffing. If the governors act correctly according to the procedures for dismissal given by the LEA then the cost of that dismissal in terms of redundancy pay, etc will be borne by the LEA and not by the school budget. This means that LEA compulsory redeployment schemes are no longer enforceable as governors will no longer be compelled to take staff. The LEA, while losing its direct control over staff, still retains the responsibility for in-service training and staff development. In terms of responsibility this leaves a paradox. While the LEA is still the employer of staff and picks up the bill in terms of redundancy pay, etc it is the governors who hire and fire them.

## WHAT IS COMPETITIVE TENDERING?

LEAs are required under the Local Government Act 1988 to put out to competitive tender the following school activities:
- Cleaning.
- Catering.
- Grounds maintenance.

As full financial delegation does not have to come in until 1993 it is likely that LEAs will accept tenders for the above on behalf of a school but that when they come up for renewal the school will be free to choose its own arrangements. Schools will then have the choice of inviting the LEA to carry out the work or of going direct to the private sector.

## TIME SCALE FOR IMPLEMENTATION

1. In September 1989 all LEAs will have submitted their plans to the DES for delegated financial control in their schools.
2. Failure to comply will result in an **imposed scheme** by the Secretary of State.
3. Schemes must be fully operational by April 1993 in all primary schools with over 200 pupils and all secondary schools.
4. LEAs have to describe how they will phase the implementation of the scheme.

Within this framework the important things for an LEA to do are:
- Set up consultation mechanisms with governors, teachers, etc.
- Develop a formula.
- Develop management and financial information systems for schools.
- Establish training schemes for LEA and school staff and governors.
- Establish pilot schools to evaluate and monitor the impact of formula funding, etc.

## A NEW WAY OF THINKING

We need to have in mind two main points about LMS before proceeding further:

# What is Local Management of Schools?

1. The role of budgeting in the education cycle.
2. The role of delegated finance in view of other changes in the education system.

These are important because the authors believe that the way in which LMS is viewed has a significant impact on the way it is managed.

## THE ROLE OF BUDGETING IN THE EDUCATION CYCLE

Money facilitates the education process and it is important that schools view it in this way. The following diagram shows a school management cycle:

### SCHOOL MANAGEMENT CYCLE

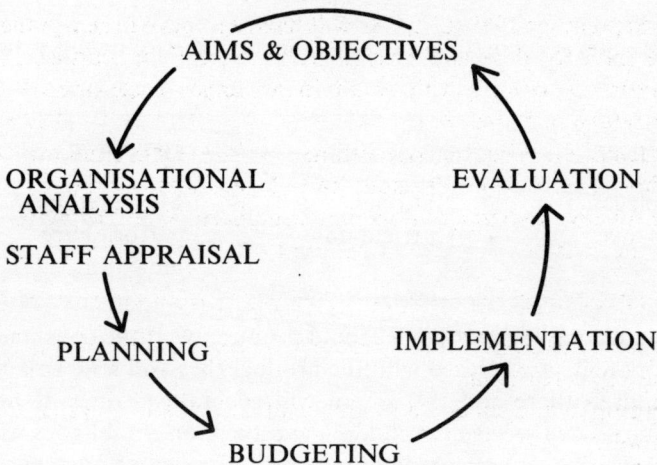

Schools will have clear aims and objectives, will assess their organisational and staffing resources, will plan their curriculum and have budgetary flexibility to get the best mix of resources. Once they have implemented their plans they will obviously evaluate the results and start the cycle again. Thus finance and budgeting should not be seen as a separate activity but as part of the cycle of school management activities.

## DELEGATED FINANCE AND OTHER CHANGES

Delegated finance should be considered alongside:

- **formula funding** – where money follows the number of pupils on roll plus other factors.
- **open enrolments** – where parents can choose the school they want their children to attend.
- **staffing delegation** – where governors decide the level of staffing once the number of pupils determines the amount of the budget.
- **performance indicators** – assessing a school on criteria, one of which is good financial management.

These factors will be considered in more detail in later chapters, but it can already be seen that schools which deliver what parents want in terms of education will gain more pupils and hence more money and can afford more staff. This is very much a market model of education.

In this market orientated view of education the following would be true:

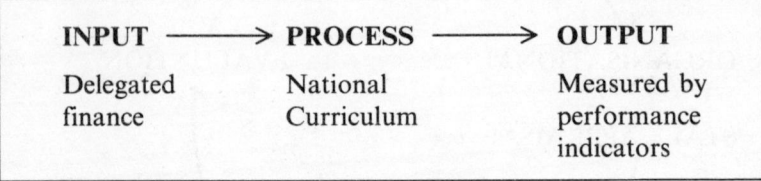

| INPUT → | PROCESS → | OUTPUT |
|---|---|---|
| Delegated finance | National Curriculum | Measured by performance indicators |

Schools under a market system should produce what the consumers want. If parents are pleased with the product they will send or keep their children there and the school will generate income. If not, other schools will receive the children and the money that goes with them. Thus schools are competing through a policy of open enrolments to generate pupils and funds. If they succeed they can take on more staff. If not they will have to reduce staffing levels. The assessment of a 'good' school takes place on a formal level with performance indicators and on an informal level with the parental 'grapevine'. This is a very different view of what a school system is than we have been used to.

This chapter has outlined the nature and dimensions of the change in financial control in schools. It has also shown ways of thinking about budgeting. The context of this change provides an important framework in which to set the material that comes in the following chapters. Chapter Two reviews the experience of delegation to date from pilot schemes and highlights seven key areas that will be developed later.

# 2
# Experience of LEA Schemes to Date

Delegating financial control to schools can be traced back as far as Hertfordshire in the early 1950s, but this was very limited and did not develop very far. The first significant move was in the early 1970s with the ILEA's **Alternative Use of Resources** scheme (AUR). This gave schools limited control over staffing and other parts of their budget. Authorities such as Cheshire (in the mid-1970s) developed schemes where schools had control of *non*-staffing resources, with the intention of evolving so that schools could take greater and greater control of their budgets. More radical approaches of LEAs such as Cambridgeshire and Solihull have led to schools having control of 85% to 95% of the school budget. These have been the forerunners of many LEA attempts in the early 1980s to set up pilot schools with total autonomy to assess the delegated approach.

What has experience shown to be the key aspects of these experimental schemes? Seven items have emerged as significant factors in the LMS debate. These are:

- Resource distribution mechanism: the formula.
- Management approaches and skills.
- Management information systems and administrative support.
- The role of the LEA.
- The role of the governors.
- Training.
- Benefits of delegated financial control.

**RESOURCE DISTRIBUTION MECHANISM: THE FORMULA**

In the early pilot schemes such as Cambridgeshire and Solihull resources were distributed on an historical cost basis. The LEA had used the existing budget base and adjusted it for minor changes in the following year. This incremental approach has provided certainty and stability in planning. It has also allowed the LEA to fund fixed costs of buildings and variable costs of pupil-led expenses such as staffing separately. It has also meant that staff salaries are paid on actual costs and not on average salary costs (a point developed later).

The critics of historical costing argue that it merely reinforces past spending patterns and mistakes and does not force schools to re-appraise what they are doing. It also does not allow schools to make alternative decisions on real resource costs; only on artificial historical ones.

The move, both in current schemes such as Cambridgeshire and Solihull and under the Government's proposal, is towards distributing resources by a formula mainly related to the age and number of pupils—although it can be weighted (marginally) by other factors.

The problem with a formula based solely on pupil numbers is that it can be very harmful to small schools, whose fixed costs take up so much of their budget. This will be demonstrated in Chapter Three.

Solihull developed quite a sophisticated formula profile. It included building maintenance based on the capital value of the school, fuel costs according to historical consumption patterns and current costs, grounds maintenance based on acreage and staffing determined by pupil numbers. This sophisticated formula profile is unlikely to survive the Government's requirements. On completing its five year pilot scheme in 1987 Cambridgeshire ran into problems when moving away from historical cost to formula-based funding. It was faced with the choice between a curriculum-led model called 'organization-based staffing' (which funded the schools according to their curricular needs and thus compensated smaller schools) or a pupil number based scheme called 'average-weighted pupil numbers'. The Council opted for the latter because it was cheaper.

A further complication with the framework proposed by the Government is that schools will be given staffing funds based on the average cost of a teacher but will be charged the actual cost of the staff in the school. This means that schools with older staff who are at the top end of the incremental salary scales will have inadequate finance while schools with a younger age profile will gain finance.

The Audit Commission (1988) compares two schools with a similar number of pupils which might employ 30 staff each. It calculates that one with relatively inexperienced teachers could pay

£377,610 in salaries while the other with a more experienced staff would pay £426,180. This could lead to teacher sackings and governors not being able to afford to keep all their staff.

As schools move away from incremental historical budgets towards formula-based ones they will be forced to take a fresh view of which resources to employ. This is often called a zero-based review.

## MANAGEMENT APPROACHES AND SKILLS

### Objective setting

Which management skills are needed and which are in fact being developed? Experience of pilot schemes to date suggests that schools with clear aims and objectives are able to allocate resources to meet them. Schools without such clear objectives tend to follow an incremental approach and do not use the resource flexibility that delegation offers to a school.

Therefore, an initial key factor is that schools should have clear aims and objectives if resource provision is to be harnessed to meet those needs. Schools will clearly be expected to produce **management plans** to articulate these objectives.

### Participation

A second key issue is the management of effective decision-making within the school. Davies (1987) sees:

> "Participation in decision-making is also an important area to consider... If one applies this delegated argument within the school, should middle management and the classroom teacher be involved in determining spending because they are closer to the children and thus perceive their needs on a day to day basis."

The *Coopers and Lybrand Report* (1988) suggests that delegating more power to the school means that decision-making in the school takes on greater importance. This is especially important when establishing a school management team to be involved in the decision-making process. Setting up good decision-making structures with the right staff participation emerges as a management skill and task to be developed.

### Financial and planning skills

A third area is technical skill—understanding and interpreting budgets. The *Coopers and Lybrand Report* (1988) states:

> "Each school will then be faced with the task of planning its operations to achieve educational objectives within the constraints of the cash limits... budgets developed at this stage should contain proposals with estimated costs for curriculum and extra-curricular costs and other expenses."

Because of this, planning and budgeting skills need to be developed.

## MANAGEMENT INFORMATION SYSTEMS AND ADMINISTRATIVE SUPPORT

The nature of administrative support—an effective management information system (MIS) and back-up staff—is a key issue that emerges from the pilot schemes.

The problem with most LEA administration systems is that they deal with total budgets; it is a completely different matter to provide detailed school-centred information. If the information is not complete or accurate the school will not be able to make re-allocation (virement) or any other decisions.

In the cases of Solihull and Cambridgeshire neither LEA provided any more money to pay for additional clerical support. However, some schools in both these LEAs have used 'savings' in other areas of the budget to hire additional clerical staff to run the scheme.

Two points emerge from reports in this area. Firstly, LEA financial information which was aggregated for all its schools has to be disaggregated. It then has to be provided to individual schools in an efficient, comprehensible, accurate and reliable way so that management decisions can be based on correct information. Secondly, extra support staff time is needed to cope with the administration and this often has to be paid for by savings elsewhere.

## THE ROLE OF THE LEA

With delegation the LEAs' role will become a more strategic one, in that it will be setting policy and parameters but leaving detailed implementation to the schools (while still monitoring performance). The Government's view is that LEAs will have a vital overall responsibility for ensuring that schemes of delegation are effective in delivering better education.

The Government sees the LEA as having these key responsibilities. It will:

- Determine the total resources available to schools.
- Decide the scope of delegation within the framework of the Act.
- Establish the basis for allocating resources to individual schools.
- Set out the conditions and requirements within which governing bodies must operate.
- Monitor the performance of schools and give advice to take corrective action if necessary.
- Operate sanctions, including withdrawal of delegation, if required.

(DES *Draft Consultative Document: Financial Delegation to Schools*, 7/1988).

## THE ROLE OF GOVERNORS

In North America financial power is delegated to the head (principal), but under pilot schemes in England and under the new Government proposals **financial power is delegated to the governors** of the school. The 1986 Education Act reorganised governing bodies from September 1988 giving greater power to parents and less to local political groups. It also gave governing bodies the right to appoint and dismiss staff, a responsibility previously reserved for the LEA.

Delegation to governors is intended to enhance the involvement of parents and the wider community. They will work with teachers and the LEA to provide an education that the 'consumers' want. How this works out in practice remains to be seen.

## TRAINING

Most commentators see the success of delegation of financial control as depending on the adequate training of heads, staff and governors in their new roles and responsibilities. The earlier schemes of Cambridgeshire and Solihull have proceeded by 'trial and error'. This has not produced the disasters that opponents expected, mainly because a few pilot schools can receive significant informal support from the LEA, something that is not possible on a large scale.

As an effective scheme for training heads and staff, Davies (1988) puts forward a systematic and comprehensive training programme in three stages for LEAs to implement. These stages involve:

1. An initial familiarisation with the nature and dimensions of the change.
2. A detailed development of management strategies and skills to manage delegated finance.
3. Technical MIS skills and team building.

## THE BENEFITS OF DELEGATED FINANCIAL CONTROL

Clearly, changes will take place in the roles of those in the Education Service involved in delegated finance and some functional processes (such as management information systems) need to be perfected. But what are the benefits and failures of the experience to date?

Most headteachers in the pilot schemes have agreed that better decisions are made by those closely involved with the children. They also consider that they are getting better value for money as they can match needs and resources more closely. Being more flexible with resources has encouraged schools to plan ahead and change things.

A head of a junior school in Solihull appointed extra part-time staff and bought extra resources out of savings. In Cambridgeshire none of the seven original pilot schools has tried to make savings in staffing. They have given priority to teachers, support staff and books and equipment. Other advantages emerge from the pilot schemes: governors felt more involved with their schools; staff morale increased as more resources become available; decisions were made and jobs finished more quickly. This leads to savings in time, energy and temper.

Experience to date suggests that pilot schemes in LEAs such as Cambridgeshire and Solihull have shown benefits that overcome some of the costs involved in running these schemes.

## SUMMARY

This review of experience to date suggests seven key factors:

- Resource distribution mechanism: the formula.

- Management approaches and skills.
- Management information systems and administrative support.
- The role of the LEA.
- The role of the governors.
- Training.
- Benefits of delegated financial control.

These are key factors to which in any well run school careful attention will have to be paid if LMS is to be a success. We focus in the next chapter on financial information and management which will consider elements of the first three factors.

# 3
# School Costs and School Budgets

This Chapter will examine a number of key issues:

- The nature of school costs and the formula.
- The school budget – items of expenditure: primary and secondary.
- The type of financial and management information necessary: record systems.
- The use of information technology.
- Virement and virement strategies.
- Who takes financial decisions.
- The key management factor.

## THE NATURE OF SCHOOL COSTS AND THE FORMULA

Before looking at the details of school budgets let us stand back and take a strategic look at the nature of school costs and the importance of the formula funding system to them. (Formula funding means money is distributed according to the number of pupils and other quantitative factors.)

School costs can be divided into two broad categories—fixed costs and variable costs.

- **Fixed costs** are those that the school will have to pay regardless of the number of pupils on roll. If a primary school suffered a decline in pupils from 200 to 180 or a secondary school from 1,100 to 1,050 it would still have to meet its fixed costs. A good example of this would be the maintenance of the building and a minimum level of heating to prevent frost damage in winter.
- **Variable costs** are those which will increase or decrease according to the number of pupils on roll. For example the more pupils in a school the more teachers are needed, and the more text and exercise books.

This is a rather simplistic dividing of expenditure; in the real world some expenditure would have both fixed *and* variable elements. A school which employed a caretaker could regard this as a fixed cost while if he was paid overtime for cleaning up for after-school activities this would be variable expenditure. Generally, premises-related costs tend to have a very high fixed cost element: teaching and supply costs have a high variable cost element.

In the English education system the proportion of expenditure going on fixed and variable costs differs from school to school and LEA to LEA. However a rough average would suggest that 70% of expenditure is variable and 30% is fixed in schools operating at or near their pupil capacity.

The following diagram shows a situation where school funding is determined by pupil numbers only (in the 1988 Act it is a minimum of 75 per cent).

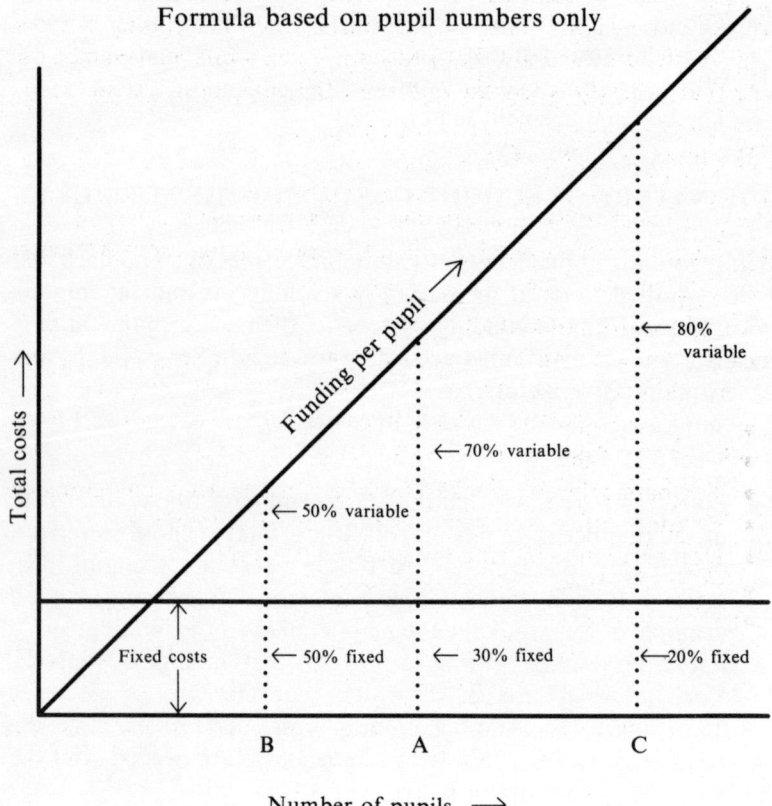

A school at point A will be spending 70% of its budget on variable costs such as teachers, books and equipment, and 30% of its budget on fixed costs, mainly premises. If it gains pupils the money they bring in will not have to be spent on fixed costs (the buildings are already maintained) and most of it can be spent on more teachers, books and equipment. So at point C although it spends the same amount on its fixed costs they are now a smaller proportion of total costs.

The reverse is true when a school loses pupils. Although it gets less money it still has to meet its fixed costs. As a result these fixed costs take up a bigger share of the budget, leaving less to spend on the variable costs of teachers and materials.

Thus, with open enrolments, where parents can choose which school their children go to, the movement of pupils between schools will have a big effect on budgets. Expanding schools will be able to spend much of their income on teachers and materials and so attract more pupils. The reverse will be true of declining schools. This reinforces the point that LMS is not just a financial change but one that radically alters the nature of the education system.

## THE SCHOOL BUDGET

### Items of expenditure: primary and secondary schools

The items of expenditure for which a school will be responsible were listed in Chapter One as:

- Buildings – internal maintenance.
- Equipment – furniture and fittings; specific educational equipment.
- Rent and rates.
- Fuel and light.
- Textbooks, library books, stationery, materials and equipment.
- Printing, office stationery, postage and telephone.
- Domestic and cleaning materials and equipment.
- Staff travelling, educational visits.
- Examination fees.
- Staffing – teachers, technicians, classroom assistants, secretarial and administration staff.

For the sake of convenience these can be grouped under five broad headings of expenditure and one of income.

- Employee costs.
- Premises-related costs.
- Supplies and services.
- Establishment expenses.
- Miscellaneous expenses.
- Income generated.

Thus a detailed budget would look like this:

**Primary School Budget**
*Employee costs*
| | |
|---|---:|
| Teachers | £174,080 |
| Supply cover | £2,800 |
| Support staff | £10,848 |
| Caretaker & cleaners | £11,100 |

*Premises costs*
| | |
|---|---:|
| Building maintenance | £5,200 |
| Grounds maintenance | £1,300 |
| Gas | £6,230 |
| Electricity | £1,700 |
| Water | £510 |
| Cleaning materials | £600 |
| Rates | £9,950 |

*Supplies and services*
| | |
|---|---:|
| Capitation | £3,660 |

*Establishment expenses*
| | |
|---|---:|
| Postage | £110 |
| Printing and stationery | £300 |
| Telephone | £600 |
| Travelling allowances | £257 |
| Staff advertising | £100 |

*Miscellaneous*
| | |
|---|---:|
| Staff training | £700 |

– can't be transferred (vired)-
o another area

*Income*
| | |
|---|---:|
| Letting of Hall | £600 |

**Secondary School Budget**
*Employee costs*
| | |
|---|---:|
| Teachers | £1,211,589 |
| Supply cover | £14,110 |
| Support staff | £65,324 |
| Caretaker & cleaners | £54,011 |

*Premises costs*
| | |
|---|---:|
| Building maintenance | £25,200 |
| Grounds maintenance | £6,356 |
| Gas | £26,239 |
| Electricity | £11,754 |
| Water | £1,510 |
| Cleaning materials | £3,400 |
| Rates | £85,410 |

*Supplies and services*
| | |
|---|---:|
| Capitation | £50,440 |

*Establishment expenses*
| | |
|---|---:|
| Postage | £850 |
| Printing and stationery | £2,400 |
| Telephone | £4,000 |
| Travelling allowances | £2,857 |
| Staff advertising | £540 |

*Miscellaneous*
| | |
|---|---:|
| Staff training | £3,000 |

– can't be transferred (vired)-
o another area

*Income*
| | |
|---|---:|
| Letting of Hall | £2000 |

## MANAGEMENT AND FINANCIAL INFORMATION SYSTEMS

Information needs to be clearly presented for management purposes. For example:

| 1 Budget total for the year | 2 Expected expenditure by this date | 3 Committed expenditure by this date | 4 Actual expenditure by this date | 5 Variation between expected & committed expenditure to date |
|---|---|---|---|---|
| | | | | |

### Example

To show this in a practical example we will use three examples of expenditure at the end of January, ten months through the financial year (see table overleaf).

### What do these figures tell us?

Firstly, if we look at teachers' salaries in the table overleaf the school is not employing its full complement of teachers during the year. It has not employed a part-time teacher one day a week for most of the year. This means that it has a surplus in this budget of £1,994 to re-allocate. The reason that the committed expenditure in column 3 and actual expenditure in column 4 are the same is that the school has committed this expenditure and the LEA has actually paid this money out in salaries.

Secondly, let us look at the budget for supply teachers (replacement for absent teachers). Of the original allocation of £2,800, part of it (£1,500) has been committed, that is, supply teachers engaged. However, because of delays in paying their claims forms only £1,200 of this £1,500 has actually been paid. When they have been paid for this work done, £833 will still be left out of the money that was expected to be spent by this date.

Thirdly, capitation shows that the school exceeded its expected expenditure to date of £3,050 by sending out orders of £3,800 (committed expenditure). It has also committed more than its original budget allocation.

| | 1 Budget Total for the year | 2 Expected expenditure to date | 3 Committed expenditure to date | 4 Actual expenditure to date | 5 Variation between expected & committed expenditure |
|---|---|---|---|---|---|
| | £ | £ | £ | £ | £ |
| Teachers' salaries | 174,080 | 145,967 | 143,073 | 143,073 | 1,994 − |
| Supply teachers | 2,800 | 2,333 | 1,500 | 1,200 | 833 − |
| Capitation | 3,660 | 3,050 | 3,800 | 3,000 | 750 + |

## School Costs and Budgets

A number of points are worth emphasising:

1. 'Committed to date' figures are just as important as actual expenditure. Because of the delays in paying bills, schools *must* act on what they have committed to spend and not on the bills actually paid. This is like a person writing a cheque. Because the £900 cheque has not been presented and the bank account shows £1,000 balance it would be wrong to think that there is £1,000 to spend. Once the cheque reaches the bank the balance goes down to £100.
2. The 'expected expenditure to date' figures are obtained by dividing the actual budget by 12 months so that in the first month the figure is one twelfth. In our example the figure is ten twelfths as we are ten months through the financial year.
3. The reason for the 'expected to date' and the 'committed to date' figures is that if there is a difference then action can be taken that month and not at the end of the financial year. (Virement is looked at later in this chapter.)
4. Overspending and underspending on individual items are relatively unimportant; it is the total over- or underspending that needs consideration. So, in our example the overspending on capitation is more than compensated for by other items underspent.
5. Schools should not plan to underspend to any significant extent to play safe! Inflation makes it less valuable to use the money in the following year. Underspending may also demonstrate to local politicians that schools don't need all their money.
6. Scale of expenditure is very important. If a primary school has a budget of £280,000 and a secondary school £1,500,000, should a lot of management time be used worrying about an underspend or overspend of £500? This is a difficult change of attitude for headteachers who have previously managed very small amounts of money.

It is important that the record system based on computers or paper given to schools by the LEA should have the five headings of expenditure described. It is upon this sort of easily understood practical information that decisions can be made. It goes without saying that the information should be accurate and reliable as well as up to date. The practical success of LMS will depend on it meeting these criteria.

## THE USE OF INFORMATION TECHNOLOGY

There are a number of ways of keeping records and producing a management and financial information system under the five headings discussed above.

Obviously schools can keep manual paper-based systems. However, the advent of information technology should provide a much more efficient and effective method. One solution is to link the central LEA computer system to the schools with terminals in each school. A second is to provide a school with a microcomputer with software which will perform certain administrative tasks. These could be pupil record systems, wordprocessing, timetabling, exam entries and a financial management package.

The second option seems to be proving more popular. This means that the schools will have to keep their own record system and reconcile it with the LEA central system. This is similar to individuals reconciling their cheque book (their record system) with the bank statement received each month (the bank's record system).

Pioneering work done by Bedfordshire to develop a **Schools Information and Management System** (SIMS) has produced a commercially available software package for financial and other administration in schools. IBM, working with Cambridgeshire, has also produced some excellent software programs including a financial package that will run school budgets.

It is important that an LEA adopts a standard administrative system for school finance so that it can have a consistent and comprehensive approach to training and the application of the new technology in this area.

## VIREMENT AND VIREMENT STRATEGIES

Virement simply means moving around; money can be moved (vired) from one budget area to another. In a sense, as long as a school is operating within its total budget, the amount it spends on each individual item is less important. Thus, a deficit of £500 in one budget area can be rectified by viring money from a budget area in surplus.

This can be of tremendous benefit to schools. Under traditional systems of finance, if during a mild winter a school did not spend all its heating budget then the saving was retained by the LEA. Now the saving stays in the school and can be spent in other areas. This is true of such areas as staffing. A school that cannot get a supply teacher and covers the absence itself does at least keep the supply teacher's salary to spend on books, equipment, etc.

In our earlier example (of teachers' salaries, supply cover and capitation) it is important that the managers of a school, before they vire money, are confident that the information on which they base their decisions is correct. This is why the *committed* figure is important and not just actual payments made. If the information is correct then monthly monitoring should result in money being moved from one expenditure area to another as necessary. This should take place during the year as surpluses and deficits reveal themselves: it should not be left to the end of the financial year.

If, in our example, there are surpluses of £1,994 on teachers' salaries, £833 on supply cover and a £750 overspend on capitation, the following factors should be taken into account:

1. The surplus on teachers' salaries is a clear case for reallocation as the school will know that it is not using all its part-time teaching allocation and this is a planned underspend.

2. The allocation for supply teachers, although underspent, is still having to fund the remaining two months of the financial year, February and March, both of which are high illness and absence months. Therefore it may be better only to re-allocate part of this money and to keep some in reserve.

3. The capitation in most schools is spent by this time of the year. One of the problems of a system which demands ten twelfths of the money to be spent by the end of January is that it is only fully effective for items such as salaries which are paid in twelve equal monthly instalments. With capitation one may expect all the money to be spent by the end of January, so the overspend may be the final one of £3,800 − £3,660 = £140. In this case minor amounts like this can easily be balanced off from other areas.

4. Interpreting the figures is so important. The figures themselves do not make the virement decisions; it is the head and governors who assess their reliability and importance along with other background factors before decisions are made.

## WHO TAKES FINANCIAL DECISIONS?

Later in Chapter Six we look at participation of staff, the role of governors and the role of the head in this area. It is important that one person alone does not take decisions affecting the number of staff employed, the working conditions of staff and pupils and the books and materials used. Full involvement in setting the aims and objectives of the school and considering their financial implications has to take place if the background to the financial decisions is to be understood.

Governors and senior staff must set up a structure to make the difficult decisions about what can be afforded once the broad parameters of the school's objectives and the financial limitations have been set. It is often recommended by management consultants that organisations should plan to spend 105% of budgets and then decide between alternatives to reduce the budget down to 100%. This encourages the development of options and alternatives and schools can be led by curriculum needs. Starting purely from financial limitations is very restricting on the imagination and creativity of organisations.

## THE KEY MANAGEMENT FACTOR

Throughout this chapter we have been looking at items of expenditure under different budget headings. Traditionally the LEA has given a school an allocation in each of these. In future a school will not have an amount for 'staffing' and an amount for 'capitation'; it will have a **lump sum budget** and it will determine how much goes under each budget heading. It will determine the level of staffing, capitation etc within the overall budget constraints. This is a very radical change in the role and power of the governors and head.

# 4
# Managing the School Budget

The exact form of each school's delegated budget will be decided by its local education authority. Each LEA will make up its own formula for the funding that schools receive. The LEAs have been given detailed guidance to help them create their own formula by the Education Reform Act and by two lengthy DES circulars. Even so, there remain a number of discretionary areas which will be included in schools' budgets from the start of LMS by some authorities and not by others. Equally, interpretation of the legislation will vary according to local circumstances and practices. What will be common, however, are the management issues that will arise regardless of these regional differences.

The LEAs, then, are required to delegate the lion's share of school budgets. This includes:

- Employee costs.
- Premises related costs.
- Supplies and services.
- Establishment expenses.
- Miscellaneous expenses.

This much will be standard, and will now be discussed in more detail.

## MANAGING EMPLOYEE COSTS

The day-to-day clerical administration of schools' payrolls is still likely to be done by the LEAs, but the composition of those payrolls will be decided by the schools themselves. Under the legislation, the governing bodies of schools with delegated budgets will control the level of staffing. This applies both to teaching and non-teaching staff. Therefore, the governing body (or in some circumstances its sub-committee) will control appointments, discipline and grievance procedures, and dismissals within the school. Such powers are without parallel in any other education system in Western Europe.

Advice about staffing may be given by the LEAs on a number of issues such as:

- Headteacher or deputy headteacher appointments.
- Appointment of other teachers.
- Appointment of non-teaching staff.

In each case, the governing body can decide to ignore the advice of the LEA, but once appointed the member of staff becomes an employee of the local authority, rather than of the school.

## MANAGING TEACHING STAFF COSTS

Usually the headteacher is expected to play a significant, if not dominant, role in all staffing matters. In a well run school the management plan should clearly indicate how many teachers are needed to deliver the curriculum. In schools which have not been planning ahead historical staffing data may be called upon to show the teacher numbers required, assuming a static curriculum and a steady pupil number on roll. The key point remains that the number of teachers that schools can employ will depend on what percentage of their budgets can be allocated for teachers' salaries.

This area of staffing highlights much of the debate concerning efficiency and effectiveness within schools. In seeking efficiency schools may become concerned with delivering the same education at less expense, while effectiveness would seek to achieve a high quality of educational provision. Efficiency places the emphasis on cost, effectiveness on desired outcome.

In many cases headteachers will have to decide between these two competing demands. For example, by delaying a secondary school appointment for a term a saving of several thousand pounds would be made. Savings of this type could then be consolidated if a probationary or licensed teacher were to be employed to fill the vacancy rather than an experienced professional. In either case the class would have a teacher in front of them. Efficiency might suggest that the cheaper teacher should be appointed, although this could reduce the quality of education provided.

Equally, in a primary school an increase in the teaching load of the headteacher could save several thousand pounds a year. This would equal the entire capitation allowance received previously by many schools in this sector. However, effective management of the school could suffer under such circumstances.

Very similar arguments are likely to be voiced under LMS in connection with incentive allowances. These extra payments are given to teachers who

- Have extra responsibilities, or
- Are outstanding classroom teachers, or
- Teach a subject where there is a shortage of teachers, or
- Work in a post which is difficult to fill.

Under the legislation the governing body is likely to receive discretionary powers on incentive allowances to be used within a school. Provided they stay within the broad outlines of the *School Teachers' Pay and Conditions* document governors can decide how many teachers will be paid on the higher pay rates known by the letters 'A' to 'E'. Equally a large secondary school could decide between having two and four deputy headteachers. Based on present salary scales, if two deputies in such a school retired and were replaced by two teachers on 'E' allowances, over £10,000 would be saved. At the other end of the spectrum, in a Group 4 primary school, in order to achieve effective curriculum leadership it might be thought advisable to have half the staff receiving incentive allowances at an additional cost of about £4,500. Alternatively, such a sum would buy in a part-time teacher or full-time extra secretarial assistance.

LMS will give headteachers the chance to offer their governing bodies a wide range of choices in relation to staffing costs, but they will first have to consider educational requirements. The danger of advocating cost reductions rather than educational effectiveness is very real, particularly if results come to be narrowly defined by assessment results. To do this is to ape the crooked tailor whose catch phrase was 'Never mind the quality, feel the width!' Economies on staffing could well lead eventually to a decline in pupil numbers, as potential clients go elsewhere. What remains critical is that teachers' expertise is optimised at all times. To achieve this requires skilful management irrespective of pressures arising from delegated finance.

## MANAGING SUPPLY TEACHERS COSTS

LEA formulas will have to consider the problem of the cost of supply teachers whose salaries fall upon the schools in the first instance.

For schools there are a number of potentially expensive options which have to be resolved. Firstly, if a teacher is absent, the school will have to pay for a replacement. This will lead to it paying twice for the teaching done on that particular day. Equally, in the event of long term sickness or maternity leave the school would have to pay the salary costs of the replacement teacher as well as those of the original. Both these problems have been recognised and await local solutions since LEAs have discretionary powers over this expend-iture item. They may decide either to keep money centrally for supply staff or else to include this in the delegated budgets of schools.

In large schools it may be possible to cover absences internally, ploughing the savings back to departmental funds. Smaller schools look particularly vulnerable, and the prospect of primary head-teachers spending more of their time providing cover for absent teachers is very real. One way of resolving this would be to make more use of 'floating' teachers who would normally be used to support the curriculum throughout the school, but upon whom headteachers could make the first call in these circumstances. However, any such cover would have to be paid for, and would almost certainly lead to larger class sizes in the rest of the school.

## MANAGING NON-TEACHING STAFF COSTS

The way in which appointments for non-teaching staff will be made is very similar to that for teaching staff. When a new post has been created it will be up to the governors to decide at which level or grade the position should be recorded.

Notwithstanding the comments made above on effectiveness $v$. efficiency, it may be possible to rationalise some of the work of teachers in schools and employ cheaper ancillaries to do the same tasks. One obvious example is the administration that LMS will produce. Much of this will involve necessary, but low level, book-keeping skills. It would smack of mismanagement for a headteacher to become involved in this type of work, just as it is presently ridiculous for headteachers to spend their mornings counting up their schools' dinner money. Many secondary schools are therefore likely to employ bursars or registrars to maintain their financial systems for them. They could employ people with book-keeping skills and common sense for this work rather than more highly paid teachers and managers.

Teachers in secondary schools might be encouraged to work an extra period if they knew that their department could then afford a part-time secretary to free them from the tyranny of the photocopier, banda machine and telephone. Such choices under the logic of LMS should not be made solely by the senior management team within schools, but by the teachers personally affected by their decisions.

## MANAGING PREMISES-RELATED COSTS

This is the second major area of new responsibility for schools under LMS. The new relationship between the school and LEA may be thought of as similar to that between landlord and tenant. So the school becomes responsible for the payment of rates, and where necessary any rent associated with non-LEA property. Under the same notion, the school becomes responsible for internal maintenance.

Circular 7/88 from the DES suggests how LEAs might divide responsibility for the maintenance of school buildings, but this area is one where there is likely to be some ambiguity. For example if a school wished to restyle toilet facilities, they might expect the LEA to replace the sanitary equipment, even though this would be inside the building. The rest of the decoration would be the responsibility of the school and would be paid for from the school's delegated funds. However, suppose the local authority does not agree to replace the equipment; the school is left to abandon the project or take on the full costs itself. There may also be situations where poor external maintenance affects the internal decoration and in these cases the school would have to seek recompense from the LEA.

Nor can the school ignore legislation and LEA policies on health and safety. Some matters may fall to the governing body: the purchase and maintenance of fire-fighting equipment, cleaning and non-structural repairs. However local LMS schemes will have to say where the responsibility lies. If for example a window is broken, the circular suggests that the school should replace the glass, but that the LEA should pay for any external repainting as part of their brief to maintain the external fabric.

Managers in schools are likely to spend more and more time negotiating with local authorities in areas where responsibility is vague. This is one area of possible conflict likely to strain the emerging relationships which LEAs will have to develop with their schools if they wish to keep their influence.

In many other areas there has been a tightening up of wasteful use over the last decade as education budgets have been squeezed. Zonal heating for example has saved thousands of pounds in many schools both as a result of shutting down areas not used by children throughout the day and of allowing heating to be targeted during evening or weekend lettings. Lighting is another area where schools have tried to become more cost conscious, with mixed results. Although there may not be very much scope for savings in these, or similar areas, they need careful managing since their potential for increasing costs remains a considerable threat. The vision of an unexpectedly large heating bill wreaking havoc with careful calculations and tight margins is very real.

Another issue which will be raised over internal upkeep will be one of competence. Headteachers and other school managers may not be qualified to evaluate work carried out at the school's expense. In the past LEAs have been able to provide the necessary expertise. This may not be so easy in the future, or it may have to be paid for. A second danger here is that school managers will not be aware of improvements which could lead to considerable savings over time. As a result premise costs may be kept higher than might otherwise be the case or continual neglect may eventually lead to the need for heavy expenditure.

Before all schools are operating delegated budgets, the 1988 Local Government Act will have effectively put school cleaning, catering and grounds maintenance out to competitive tendering. After these initial four year tenders run out, it will be the responsibility of the schools to negotiate tenders for this work as well. Schools will then be able to offer contracts for competitive tendering once their existing arrangements have been honoured. When it comes to renewal, schools may choose to use LEA services or make their own arrangments. However, all existing contracts have to be honoured, and choices will therefore only slowly become available to most schools.

Headteachers will therefore need either to develop their own expertise and knowledge or to build up a network of advisers with the appropriate skills. Without these, this aspect of delegated financial responsibility, which offers considerable scope for local initiative, is likely to make little long term impact.

## MANAGING ESTABLISHMENT EXPENSES

Many schools are used to paying for certain supplies and services out of their capitation allowances. Educational supplies and office materials have in the past accounted for the lion's share of such funds. Along with this some LEAs have already delegated control of some costs, such as telephone bills and cleaning equipment. Others, such as insurance policies, have more usually been organised by the local authority.

New services may become desirable from a marketing viewpoint. For example, it may become viable to provide transport to schools from neighbouring areas, to help parents get their children to their preferred school. The costs of any such service could simply be passed on to the parents, with the proviso that transport could not be offered unless it covered the cost.

Other services which the LEAs now provide may also in time feature in delegated budgets. The most likely ones are peripatetic and advisory teachers. If this happened then those schools that wished to offer music would have to pay for the services of the music teachers who came in to teach children. Equally, advice from LEA advisory teachers could be bought in, or purchased from other sources, such as HE providers or independent consultants.

## MANAGING SUPPLIES AND SERVICES

Most schools are very experienced at dealing with the capitation allowance for books and equipment. In future this must be seen in the context of the management plan.

## MISCELLANEOUS EXPENSES

Some forms of miscellaneous expenditure are relatively easy to forecast. In secondary schools, for instance, examination fees might be included in this category. Costs associated with staff development will perhaps be more difficult to forecast, although school management plans might well include strategic planning for this area. There will also be recruitment costs to be borne by the school when vacancies occur.

Finally, contingency expenses will have to be allowed for. Many schools engaged in pilot schemes found that they were too conservative during their first years of operation. There is a danger that this experience will be repeated many times over under LMS. If this were to become common then at least two consequences follow. Firstly, the children on whom the budget ought to have been spent will be denied the benefits that ought to have come from this expenditure. Secondly, the idea in corridors of power that schools are well financed may gain popularity—and underspending will be indicated as proving the point. Governors should certainly be very wary of headteachers who are excessively cautious with their budgets, since this indicates poor management just as much as gross overspending.

More generally the choices that will be open to schools will be made greater or smaller depending upon the income that the schools receive. Therefore, the next chapter will look at how the work of headteachers in particular will be affected by the need to keep as much money as possible coming into their schools.

# 5
# Headteachers and the Management of LMS

As we have already seen schools will have much greater freedom under the new legislation, but the exercise of much wider choice is to be balanced against greater responsiveness and accountability to the outside community. Schools will compete in a market place for pupils and this will lead to the expansion of some and the closure of others.

In order to manage such changes successfully headteachers will need to adopt a perspective close to that of the chief executive of a business firm. This chapter is concerned with reviewing aspects of the work of the head which will be altered as a consequence of LMS. These growing areas of work include the management of:

- Open enrolment.
- Marketing
- Enterprise income.

Each of these will be looked at below. The effects of delegated finance schemes on other participants will be reviewed in Chapter Six.

**OPEN ENROLMENT**

Open enrolment means that parents can choose which school their children go to provided the school has places. Under the Education Reform Act schools may recruit pupils up to their **standard number**. This figure was first set down in the 1980 Education Act, and so for secondary schools is set at the number of pupils admitted in 1979. Primary schools, however, may benefit from further increases due to calculations concerned with rising 5s and nursery provision. Whilst a LEA may agree to a request from a school's governing body to increase its standard number, only the Secretary of State can allow a school's allocated figure to be lowered.

As a central part of the package of delegated finance schools will receive income directly related to their pupil numbers. So the more children a school is educating, the bigger the budget it receives. Conversely, the fewer it is educating the smaller its budget. With market forces rather than LEA admission policies deciding recruitment levels, schools have a financial incentive to move quickly to attract children onto their rolls. As was seen in Chapter Three once the ongoing costs of the school such as staff salaries and heating bills have been met, income from additional pupils can be used more flexibly to increase the quality of the education the children receive. Therefore if each child brought with it an extra £1,000, then an example based on a large primary school might run as follows:

| Class size | Budget | Teacher salary | Indirect costs | Surplus funds |
|---|---|---|---|---|
| 30 | £30,000 | £12,000 | £7,500 | £10,500 |
| 35 | £35,000 | £12,000 | £8,000 | £15,000 |

However, if numbers started to decrease, then individual classes could be running at a loss:

| Class size | Budget | Teacher salary | Indirect costs | Surplus funds |
|---|---|---|---|---|
| 20 | £20,000 | £12,000 | £6,500 | £1,500 |
| 18 | £18,000 | £12,000 | £6,300 | –£300 |
| 15 | £15,000 | £12,000 | £6,000 | –£3,000 |

So heads will need to pay close attention to the recruitment policy of their schools. Without fairly buoyant pupil numbers schools will face the grim prospect of having to cope with a declining budget. The knock-on effect of this would be to restrict the educational opportunities that can be offered. In turn, this could bring about a downward spiral in pupil recruitment, with fixed costs proving an ever increasing burden. To prevent any such pattern emerging headteachers will need to market their schools vigorously.

To recap, then, open enrolment will mean that parents can choose between schools. If a school succeeds in attracting an increasing number of children, then the curriculum should be quite well resourced. If a school fails to recruit enough pupils, then it will lose a large part of its budget, which is based on pupil numbers. If this continues for a number of years, the school is likely to close. Put another way:

*more children = more cash = better quality of education*
*fewer children = less cash = worsening education*

Like 'shaggy dog' stories the two equations keep on repeating, until the first school becomes full and the second has to be closed down.

## MANAGING MARKETING

The term marketing may be applied in education in a number of ways. Traditionally it has been associated with public relations exercises aimed at improving the school's image within its community. For example, the reputation of many schools has benefited from the work that they have done in raising money for charities. Equally much time and effort has gone into producing school booklets available to the parents of prospective pupils. More enterprising headteachers have sponsored close working relationships with local newspaper reporters so that their schools are kept in the local eye. Such activities will no doubt continue and their importance may well increase.

However, marketing will also involve a closer identification by schools of what local communities require of them. This will need to be set alongside the educational practice within each school, which may have to be altered in the light of the community's expectations. Much of the liaison work required will probably fall to the head-teacher as both the school's figurehead and spokesperson. There will be a greater call upon the interpersonal skills of headteachers both to promote the professional decisions made within their school and to listen to ideas coming from the community. This is the essence of the new client-based relationship that headteachers will need to develop in order to safeguard the financial viability of their schools.

For some schools, particularly in rural areas, this new relationship may not be as crucial as the legislation might suggest. The realistic choice of parents between schools for their children may be limited by lack of alternatives. More usually parental choice will not be restricted in this way, and this is especially true for the primary sector where provision is more localised. One yardstick that will undoubtedly be used will be the results of the assessment testing of children of 7, 11, 14 and 16 which the Government is introducing. This data is to be published and so the quality of a school's intake will be clearly reflected in the results it achieves.

In many cases this data alone will not be crucial for parents reviewing the range of schools between which they have to choose. Many will choose on the basis of other features such as the wearing of uniforms. Headteachers will need to continue this trend and concentrate on marketing their institutions in terms of their distinctive differences.

These differences may well require strategic thinking and planning. For example, given two schools with broadly comparable assessment results, parents may well opt for the one which will provide better facilities for music or sport. Alternatively the decision may hang on perceived differences in ethos or pastoral care or even on factors such as the number of bearded members of staff. Given the importance that potential clients will attach to schools' distinctive characteristics it will not be enough to allow them to emerge in a haphazard manner. Particular marketing strategies will need to be identified and then supported by subsequent decisions relating most obviously to staffing and the allocation of financial resources.

Thus, in summary, it will become critical that schools sell themselves well. New marketing strategies will require:

- Identification of community needs.
- Acceptable assessment scores.
- Distinctive identity.

In some cases slick marketing may become more important than actually providing children with a good education. The Government however believes that parents will be able to spot the difference between those heads who have mastered the patter, and those who have really put ideas into practice.

## MANAGING ENTERPRISE INCOME

In addition to the money that schools will receive from the LEA, other large amounts of money may be brought in through entrepreneurial activity. Several areas would seem to offer scope for development here, not least:

- Traditional sources of income.
- New uses for the buildings.
- New goods.
- New services.
- Sponsorship.

**Traditional sources of income**
In the past nearly every school has been involved in fund raising, often associated with the work of PTAs. Fêtes, jumble sales, Christmas fayres, car boot sales and social events are part of the calendar of many schools because they can raise large amounts of money. Equally, profits have been made through the sale to pupils of anything from crisps and stationery to ties and sweat-shirts. During the last decade thousands of pounds have been raised by some schools through covenanting schemes. In order to qualify for such covenants, schools must first register as a charity, with parents agreeing to make annual donations which qualify for tax relief. All these types of activity are likely to continue and add to school funds.

Headteachers may wish however to make a more thorough and radical review of the income-generating potential of their schools. This would involve assessing the possible earning power of plant, goods and services which might be developed, and of expertise which might produce financial returns. These areas need to be examined in a little more detail.

**New uses for the buildings**
The upkeep and maintenance of the school plant will necessarily involve substantial expenditure. So it follows that any income that can be raised through increased use of the premises will help to offset some of these costs. This would in turn benefit the educational work of the school.

Such use of premises has occurred in the past, particularly in the evenings when many community groups have based their activities in schools. It is probable that a more realistic pricing structure would be required in order to cover the **actual** costs of heating, lighting and staff overtime payments. Indeed, it is hard to see how a large school could let out any rooms unless zonal heating had been installed. While this may involve difficult local decisions there is no reason why the educational budget of a school should subsidise aerobic clubs or masonic meetings. If, on the other hand, such activities are realistically priced and so help swell the school coffers, then they should be sought out and encouraged. It may even be possible to attract some extra groups given a working knowledge of local associations and groups.

While this evening market has always been available to schools there may also be new avenues that could profitably be explored in order to raise money. The most obvious periods when the plant is underused are the school holidays. Other educational institutions have recently moved into the leisure and conference markets, and there is no reason why schools should not follow suit. Overnight accommodation, if it could be provided, would further enhance earning potential. Depending upon the clientèle, local guest houses could be called upon to join in such ventures or classrooms could be converted into dormitories. Many independent public schools have already opened up their facilities over the summer holidays.

More long term relationships might be possible in schools which have surplus space. Small businesses might be interested in being housed in a spare classroom. Other schools might be willing to hire a classroom to serve as a base for a day's study visit—and package deals might be worked out in order to include use of the host school's minibus, catering facilities and study packs.

**New goods**
Just as greater use of the school plant will lead to financial returns, so too would the development of goods that the school could provide. One obvious area of expertise which could be tapped concerns teaching materials. Teachers, ancillaries or volunteer parents could be sub-contracted to produce these for sale by the school within educational circles. Computer software is one such example; apparatus for primary science work could be another.

Under LMS in Australia schools have generated income through staff doing consultancy and in-service work. Another avenue which has been exploited there is the sale of produce by some schools. If the growing of plants or the raising of livestock are not to be threatened by the costs of heating greenhouses and of foodstuffs then some financial returns should be sought. Animals could even be sponsored by parents and friends, as they are in many zoos.

**New services**
The exploitation of services by schools again suggests scope for entrepreneurial activity. The salary costs of a full-time secretary

could be offset by work undertaken on a commercial basis, possibly during holiday periods or through a strict division of working hours. Printing, photocopying and small scale publishing ventures would again enable fuller use of the equipment that many schools already own. Other pieces of equipment might be hired out to members of the local community who would otherwise take their business elsewhere. Where catering is part of the delegated scheme it may be possible to increase income by opening up facilities to a wider clientèle. Alongside this pupils could be offered other meals, such as breakfast, to set alongside the traditional provision of lunch. Sales of ready-made packed lunches could also boost income.

Lastly, parents might pay for certain types of extra-mural activities arranged by the school for their children, such as dance, music, art or sporting clubs. Working parents in many areas would welcome an 'after-hours' service by schools which might offer such activities and also bypass the need for childminders or the latch-key syndrome.

## Sponsorship

A final avenue worth looking at is outside sponsorship. Again this already occurs to varying degrees in some schools but in most it is capable of expansion. Outside concerns and businesses are not queueing up with open cheque books to underwrite school finances. However, the climate of closer cooperation between schools and the work place, reflected by the greater representation of industry and commerce on many governing bodies, does hold out some promise of support.

In most instances, however, this assistance may come in kind rather than as cash. For example, many high street banks have encouraged their managers to offer themselves for selection on to governing bodies. The financial expertise of such recruits would no doubt prove valuable to schools grappling with delegated finances. Other companies have come to associate themselves with programmes of in-service training for teachers in local schools.

Once more the onus may fall upon the headteacher or a deputy to seek out such expertise as exists in the community at large and attempt to bring it into use on behalf of the school. Cash may also follow, but this is less likely to be as significant as help in kind.

To recap, schools have a range of choices when it comes to raising extra funds.

1. **Stick to traditional methods**, such as:
   - PTA events.
   - Sales to children.
   - Covenants.
   - Lettings, if profitable.

2. **Explore different uses for the buildings**, such as:
   - Leisure/holiday centres.
   - Small businesses.
   - Educational visit 'packages'.

3. **Produce new goods**, such as:
   - Teaching materials.
   - Computer software.
   - Small teaching apparatus.
   - In-service materials.

4. **Expand the services they provide** to include:
   - Secretarial services.
   - Printing/photocopying.
   - Rental of equipment.
   - Catering : other clients,
     other meals,
     other choices.
   - Extra-mural acitivities/clubs.
   - After school childminding service.
   - Crèche facilities.

5. **Seek sponsorship**, either as:
   - Cash.
   - Help.
   - Or both.

# 6
# Implications for Governors, LEAs and the School Community

In this chapter we will review some of the implications for other groups of people who will be affected by delegated school budgets. These include:

- Governing bodies.
- Local education authorities.
- Teachers.
- Parents.
- Pupils.
- Local community.
- Employers.

## GOVERNING BODIES

We have already seen that under the new legislation governing bodies will enjoy very considerable powers when compared to their equivalents elsewhere in Western Europe. Most obviously, it is to the governing body that schools' budgets are delegated. They are expected to identify educational priorities and policies for the school to develop and implement. Provided that their planning is consistent with the National Curriculum and that legislation is not ignored, there should be no reason why their ideas should not be worked through in practice.

Probably the most critical relationship in this new scenario will be that between the governors of a school and its headteacher. There may be an assumption on the part of the head that educational decisions will be left as the legitimate concerns of the professional educators within his or her school. Certainly, this has very largely been the working agreement on which many schools have been run to date. Under the Education Reform Act, however, the role of the governors has become such that this cosy accommodation should be left behind. The governing body is expected to create a management plan for the school, having taken such advice as they require from the professional educators. It will then become the responsibility of the staff and head to implement this plan.

The staff, and particularly the head, are likely to be more involved in creating the management plan than has just been suggested. However, it is important that everyone concerned should acknowledge the dominant position of the governing body in the new partnerships which will manage schools under LMS. This includes holding staff to account for their work performance, regardless of whether they are cleaners, teachers or headteachers. Given the governors' power to hire and fire staff the old maxim that teachers—even incompetent ones—had a job for life should become a thing of the past. Thousands of children should be released from the tyranny of bad teaching. The same will be true of headteachers. In many countries headteachers who perform inadequately are demoted or forced to resign or retire early. Given the importance of the position of head of a school, such strictures can only be welcomed as part of the education scene in this country.

Nevertheless the performance of the school will be significantly affected by the quality of the management plan that the governing body provides. The responsibility for this rests with the governors. An outline of the form that this might take will be suggested in Chapter Seven. However, the stages involved are:

- Setting the school's aims and objectives.
- Assessing the current position.
- Planning.
- Budgeting.
- Implementation.
- Evaluation.

Only through this sort of detailed planning can clear priorities and policies be established and understood by all those involved in the work of the school. Taken together, the governors' requirements for these stages should provide answers to a series of fundamental questions concerned with the school's educational activity.

- Where is the school going?
- Why?
- How it is to get there?
- Has it arrived?

Only through providing answers to such questions can governing bodies reasonably hope to run effective and well managed schools.

To achieve such a task governors will clearly need access to a considerable amount of information and help from the teaching staff. They may need to form sub-committees and working parties to help with particular aspects of the plan. Once such working parties have produced their recommendations, and these have been accepted by the governing body, then their role becomes one of monitoring and evaluating the operation of the management plan. These activities should help develop new priorities for successive years, as well as a more intimate knowledge of the headteacher's managerial success in putting the plan into effect.

**Curriculum**
Under the Education Reform Act governors are expected to provide good quality education in their schools. Their main task is to oversee the implementation of the National Curriculum. Beyond that they may specify their own priorities within the law. LEA curriculum policies may be modified as thought necessary. In this work they will be helped by LEA inspectors who will monitor schools' performances to ensure that acceptable standards are being maintained. Their reports will be made available to governing bodies.

The new powers that governors are to enjoy have been given to them so that the children in their schools can be given a high standard of education. Control of the budget and all the other associated powers are only the means to this end. If this duty is ignored then the fundamental changes that could result from the Education Reform Act will be seriously undermined.

There is some evidence to suggest that governors have been slow to take up and exercise their powers to the full. Some governors will face opposition from teachers who believe that they have a 'divine right' concerning curricular matters. Equally, they are likely to face more indirect challenges from professional educators who do not accept that the ultimate responsibility now rests with the governing body rather than with the headteacher. Governors should not be deflected from their main objective of securing for children the quality of education to which they are entitled.

If governors are to be able to make informed choices concerning the curriculum in their schools they will need to devote more time to their work. There is likely to be an extension of governor training programmes; more school visits will become necessary; sub-committees are likely to be established which will need active members and more full governors' meetings will be arranged than in the past. One of their most difficult tasks is to ensure that the views and needs of all parts of the community are given due regard when school policies are drawn up. Local communities in many areas have become diverse in the recent past so that consideration must be given to a wide range of opinions and perspectives. For governors only to enact their own prejudices may give them personal satisfaction at the expense of the school's overall welfare.

**Staffing**
The creation of a management plan gives coherence to many of the decisions that governors will have to make later on. For example, to deliver the desired curriculum it may be necessary to employ another teacher. It will then fall to the governors to decide on the nature of the appointment, whether an incentive allowance should be paid in order to attract the right person, and whether the post should be permanent or short term. Equally, their order of priorities will determine how much of the budget should be committed to maintaining the school's plant rather than to additional staffing or equipment.

Along with governors' power to appoint staff come parallel powers concerning grievances, suspension and dismissal. In the transition period which they will shortly face schools would be well advised to use the existing expertise of their LEA to help them draw up their own policies and procedures. Much remains to be resolved either by LEA schemes or by practice.

As an example the idea that a teacher can be dismissed because the school no longer needs his/her services is implicit within the thinking of LMS. However, what happens to the teacher remains unclear. The situation is further confused as school employees are employed by the LEA. If they are dismissed from one school they may then be picked up by their LEA acting as an agency for the teacher. The LEAs will however be unable to sustain a redeployment system since governors will have the right to refuse to take on staff they find unsuitable.

The loss of these LEA powers may bring disadvantages to individual teachers, but governors should be able to enhance the staffing of their own schools. Some LEAs have in the recent past operated a 'ring fence' policy where any teachers moving into a county have been unable to apply for managerial posts within schools unless they have previously worked for that authority. This pernicious policy has meant that schools have been unable to take on talented teachers who have moved into the area, and have instead had to select from within the existing county teaching force. Quality has inevitably suffered as time-serving has become more important than expertise. Female teachers have been particularly badly served by LEAs operating such policies. A more open system should therefore offer governors greater choice, and lead to more women being employed in managerial positions.

**Budgets**
Relatively few points will be made here about the governors' role in the budgeting process. No doubt they will be closely involved through the school's management plans which will identify matters needing expenditure. It is after all money which makes such plans and policies possible. Once these important decisions have been taken then the function of the governors would seem to be more of a monitoring one, ensuring that value for money is achieved, and fine-tuning the financial mechanisms. Hence, if it seems that the school is going to underspend in a financial year, or has overestimated on its contingency fund, money could be released for additional priorities already earmarked. Governors might also be involved in sudden decisions to freeze expenditure; however this seems far less likely unless forces outside the school bring about a need for such draconian moves. This may seem fanciful, but in the past school budgets have been cut during a financial year as part of authority-wide economy drives.

Beyond the initial budgeting process, the governors' role is one of monitoring. Financial accountability in schools has varied noticeably, and in some the notion of internal auditing would be alien. However, since governors will have to account externally on the budget for which they have responsibility, attention will have to be given to this task. In secondary schools, this might well be one of the functions of a bursar, while in the primary sector, school secretaries would seem the more likely alternative. The products of such labours would then be available, probably on a monthly basis, to the representatives of the governing board.

The final area where governors may well play an important role in financial affairs is connected with their collective breadth of experience. Headteachers, as schools' chief executives, will be entering some areas where their own expertise may be meagre. These could concern maintenance of the school plant, legal affairs, or even marketing. Governors will have the opportunity to draw upon their own experience in a number of such areas to enhance the quality of the team which is leading their school.

**Accountability**
Power must be exercised accountably, and governors have to answer for action within their schools. For example, they must get value for the expenditure that they authorise. Not only will their stewardship be held to account through annual reports and meetings with parents and their local communities; they will also have to provide information for their LEAs and Central Government. Governors will not be made financially liable for debts incurred by their schools (provided they act in good faith) but inappropriate management of budgets could force an LEA to remove from a school the power to control its own budget.

Teaching in schools is to come under much greater external scrutiny. In addition to the national testing system, school performance indicators will be required. This means an enhanced role for the LEA inspectorate who will monitor schools' performances in order to be assured that acceptable standards are being both maintained and built upon. Throughout there will be a new emphasis placed upon schools producing quantitative evidence on the quality of education provided. Schools, and their governing bodies, will be judged on the basis of this evidence in the future. Mechanisms will therefore have to be created by which governors can monitor the teaching quality of their schools in advance of any external assessment.

## LOCAL EDUCATION AUTHORITIES

Under LMS there will be a significant shift in power from the LEAs to the schools. Just how powerful this will leave LEAs is not yet clear, but they do still remain responsible for a number of key matters. Within their local area they must:

- Create local policies.
- Offer support.

- Advise schools.
- Monitor performance.

As can be seen from the list, the shift moves LEAs in two directions. They will become more concerned with overall strategy and policy at the expense of their direct control of detail, so they will come to exercise their power less by dictat and more by influence. This can be illustrated by looking at each aspect in the context of delegated budgets.

**Create local policies**
Local authorities will still allocate the overall education budget. One outcome of LMS is that the education lobby may find itself weakened in town and county halls. Once money is delegated to schools it may prove harder for education officers to call for additional funds because money will have to go into the general school allocation rather than be siphoned off for special projects. Thus, energetic local politicians on education committees may seek alternative areas of interest as they are unable to fund specific projects.

Once the money has been earmarked for education the LEAs will implement their local schemes, which allocate financial resources to schools. Even within the pupil-weighting framework specified by Central Government there is scope for local authorities to make judgements which will be highly significant to the schools themselves.

Primary schools are particularly vulnerable. Very few senior LEA administrators have taught in primary schools, and in most LEAs the primary sector is seen as the poor relation. For years LEAs have made decisions relating to crucial areas such as staff/pupil ratios, curriculum-led staffing, advisory support and capitation allowances which have disadvantaged younger pupils. There is little reason to suppose that these inequalities will not be perpetuated and embodied in the LEA formulas by which delegated budgets will be calculated.

**Offer support**
Part of the funding for technical support is to come from Central Government sources. The more ambitious LEAs intend to link their secondary schools with their mainframe computers. This will enable schools to have instant and accurate information about their

financial status. It will also eliminate much paperwork, as invoices will come to be dealt with electronically. This would in turn produce savings both in postal charges and in secretarial hours. The expense involved in linking primary schools to mainframe computers would be considerable, however, and so the same advantages will not become available to that sector as a whole. If individual LEAs find LMS more difficult to implement in infant and junior schools this may well reflect the bias built into their own planning.

**Advise schools**
The advisory role of the LEA relates more generally to the education of pupils in the authority's schools. Poor financial management will lead to an impoverished curriculum, and so advice will no doubt be offered to both governors and headteachers on their management plans.

LEAs also expect that schools will seek their advice because of their experience in managing school properties. For example, not every school will have easy access to an architect among the parents, yet every LEA currently employs such professionals. Lawyers are a second example. If the LEA is to maintain its personnel in such areas it will have to come to market and sell such services to the schools. If the quality of the advice is good the schools may use it. Where the price is too high, or the advice poor, schools will look elsewhere.

**Monitor performance**
The Education Reform Act gives the LEAs the task of monitoring their schools' performances both in financial and curricular matters. If governors show themselves inept at managing delegated budgets the LEA can take back control themselves. They will no doubt be extremely reluctant to do this, just as they have been reluctant to discipline overspending headteachers in the past. However such powers do exist.

Performance is also to be monitored in terms of the National Curriculum and the assessment tests which are to be introduced. Although LEA curriculum policies may be modified by the governors the LEA has the duty of checking on compliance with the National Curriculum, religious education and worship, and also the governors' curriculum policy. Reports from the LEA inspectors will be made available to school governors, to help later discussion and planning.

In this context, LEAs also retain control of the monitoring of teachers through appraisal schemes, and of their in-service training. This will enable them to give some weighting to local priorities through in-service work, alongside the areas singled out as of national significance.

To summarise, the Education Reform Act has brought about a changing relationship between schools and their LEA. Key tasks for LEAs have been identified as:

- Determining the total resources available to schools.
- Deciding the scope of delegation within the framework of the Act.
- Establishing the basis for allocating resources to individual schools.
- Setting out the conditions and requirements within which governing bodies operate.
- Monitoring the performance of schools and giving advice or taking corrective action.
- Operating sanctions, including withdrawal of delegation if required.

## TEACHERS

Teachers are faced with two opposite trends which are embodied in LMS. On the one hand the logic of LMS is that those at the chalk face should be able to make the most informed choices about resources: LMS will increase delegation within schools as teachers throughout the school are brought into decision-making. The deliverers of the curriculum are then deciding how best to resource the curriculum they will be teaching.

On the other hand LMS is seen as part of a series of events which will bring about the demise of teachers' professional autonomy. Under LMS educational risk-taking may have to be reduced since it is potentially dangerous in marketing terms. Concern for education may become less important than turning in the right sort of test results, and raising money may have a higher priority than teaching a centrally dictated curriculum.

The arguments are finely balanced, and will only become clearer once LMS has been implemented. What is more certain, however, is that teachers will have to take on the consequences of LMS swiftly. Since ultimately their jobs are at risk this may be easier than some have imagined. Certainly teachers will have to see it as part of their role to market their school in positive terms now that clients control schools' viability. It might be hoped that the quality of individual lessons will improve as self interest becomes more apparent in staffrooms. One may even hope that the time will shortly be past when parents try in vain to have anyone answer the telephone during the lunch hour.

## PARENTS

The main benefit of LMS to parents should be increased choice. As schools compete for pupils they will have to become more open about the education they are offering. The marketing claims of individual schools will be checked against published national test results and batteries of performance indicators. In addition, parents should have a greater influence through their representatives on the governing bodies who will be party to the schools' management plans.

In return the schools are likely to look to parents for more support, much of which may be financial. As new money-making ventures are introduced into schools their easiest market will be the parents of children attending. The new reality is an educational version of the parable of the talents—schools with wealthier intakes will tend to have larger budgets than those serving poorer areas. LEAs will not have the funds to compensate for such inequalities, and so financial differentiation will increase in the short term. Eventually, there will be fewer schools as market forces bring about the closure of those unable to prevent the downward spiralling of resources.

Thus under LMS parents will become the final arbiters. Like other consumer services schools will prosper or collapse depending on their ability to interest parents in what they have on offer.

## PUPILS

Given the ambiguity that exists over whether parents or pupils are the clients of the schools, greater attention will have to be paid to the concerns of children in schools. Parents will only reluctantly move children from schools where the pupils are well motivated and content. The older the children the more their views are likely to carry some weight.

This concern for pupils' welfare will however be only one part of the equation. Since schools will be judged by their results, and since these will be published locally, there is a danger that children will become pressurised to produce results favourable to their own institutions.

At first this may limit the choice of schools for pupils with learning difficulties. Schools may operate unofficial selection processes to stop such children joining in the first place. In practice this would continue policies already operated by some headteachers. Until now, however, the justification for such dubious screening has been the social mix of the school. With the publication of test scores this practice is likely to gain further popularity as part of a process of image manipulation.

A second danger for pupils will be that their curriculum will become narrowly based on the content of the assessment tests. In the primary sector this brings back memories of teaching for the 11-plus examination. More aesthetic areas of the curriculum are likely to be threatened by the difficulties involved in producing quantitative assessments of children's development.

## LOCAL COMMUNITIES

Under the Education Reform Act schools will have to pay closer attention to what their local communities require. The main problem will come in the articulation of these needs. Governors will be one avenue through which this will happen. However, other routes will need to be found if schools are to reflect the broad spectrum of local opinion. As part of their local marketing drive schools will want to listen to as many viewpoints as they can, and so to some extent the onus will be thrown back on communities to produce representative spokespeople. It seems hard to separate this from political slogans for more 'active citizenship', although as attendance at school AGMs suggests this may take some time to develop.

## EMPLOYERS

Again under the new legislation a particular role has been given to schools in relation to the needs of local employers. The relationships between schools and industry over recent years have been patchy. In some areas many links have been developed for the benefit of both partners. Elsewhere, suspicions remain.

With LMS many schools will seek to establish wider networks in the industrial and service sectors. Many will seek commercial sponsorship; nearly all will provide local businesses with contracts of some description. Hopefully some of the artificial barriers between schools and the world of work may be broken down. Given the impending shortfall in the number of pupils joining the labour market closer links will certainly have something to offer both partners in the dialogue.

**In conclusion** two points may be highlighted. First, the success of schools under LMS will be determined by many different groups of people. Collectively they represent the school's team. Only by cooperation and team work will schools be able to survive and flourish in the new, wilder environment in which they find themselves.

The second point builds upon the first. If schools are to succeed they will have to anticipate changes within their sector of the market. It will not be enough just to react to events. Once more this will involve new skills of analysis which have never been called upon in schools themselves. Under LMS survival in certain circumstances may come to depend upon them.

# 7
# Developing School Management Plans

Under the new legislation schools' budgets will be intimately linked to their pupil numbers. Thus, in the context of open enrolment, there is a critical marketing role for headteachers and their staffs. Fuller use of schools' facilities and personnel may boost their finances, but local authority funds will remain the main source of schools' incomes.

Responsibility for school finances will be delegated to the schools' governing bodies, who must use these funds to maximum effect according to their own school's particular priorities and those identified by the communities they serve. Most headteachers will be given executive authority over the day to day management of these funds, although some will have to secure it for themselves. Headteachers are certainly likely to be more accountable than hitherto, as they will be answerable either to financial sub-committees or to governing bodies as a whole. We list below the management stages a school must go through in a planning cycle as mentioned in Chapter One.

## STAGE ONE — SETTING AIMS AND OBJECTIVES

Headteachers and their senior staff will have to do much planning and preparation, before allocating any money. This will involve setting goals for their schools, including goals related to pupil outcomes and learning experiences. These goals represent the philosophical bedrock of beliefs and values to which the school aspires. They also enable needs to be identified, and priorities to be drawn up by contrasting **what is** with **what should be**. For example, one goal might be that pupils learn through direct experience whenever possible, another that parents be regularly informed about school activities and their children's progress. By applying the 'what is' formula to these statements the school can then see whether action is needed to bring practice closer into line with intentions.

Allied to, but distinct from, goal setting comes the area of policy making. Schools' policies should provide clear directions for the work within the institution and hence a framework for action. They should therefore be more than a reiteration of the school's goals but less than a list of procedures to be carried out. Clear benefits follow within schools where these general directions are explicit and carried through. Among these benefits are the greater consistency, stability and continuity which clear directions achieve. Drafting written statements of the school's goals and policies should not involve the headteacher alone; it should be a collaborative effort which reflects both the community involvement within the school and the professional expertise of teachers. The headteacher may well start the process and be closely involved in the written end product, but other stakeholders should also be able to make their distinctive contributions. At the end of these two steps the school will have broad answers to two critical questions: where is the school going, and why? In addition there will be a framework for evaluating the work of the school.

## STAGE TWO — ASSESSING THE CURRENT POSITION

This is an analysis of a school's existing resources, together with an assessment of how well it is doing. This means that a school will have to provide the governors with a report of staffing resources determined by an appraisal system, a report of the physical resources such as books, materials and equipment, and an evaluation of how successful the school has been in achieving its objectives to date, by reference to its assessment and evaluation procedures. The governors will also need a report on the physical fabric of the school. Only when the school has decided where it wants to go and has evaluated its existing organisational resources can it move on to the next stage.

## STAGE THREE — PLANNING

It is only once the two prerequisite stages have been made that the third stage of detailed planning can be undertaken. The governing body may wish to be highly involved in both of these preliminary stages, ensuring that the community at large has a real impact on the life of the school. Even so, both exercises are crucial if schools are to avoid the practice of 'muddling through'.

**Staffing resources**
Detailed planning involves translating of policies into the curriculum that takes place in the classroom. Competent staffing is the first prerequisite for successful delivery in the classroom. Secondary schools have a tradition of curriculum-led staffing and so should be accustomed to matching the expertise of teachers to the content required in the classroom. Under LMS this matching needs to be continued and extended as far as possible. Covering of absences, as always, presents particular difficulties if the quality of classroom work is not to suffer. In addition, market forces will necessitate a tight correlation between teachers' specialisms and the number of pupils requiring particular subjects and options. Surpluses of, for example, history or classics teachers would leave a school with inappropriate staff. This would lead either to a need to employ more teachers, more periods being taught by non-specialists masquerading as experts or an increased workload for specialist staff. None of these three alternatives is acceptable at present, although additional payment for extra periods worked by staff may become a possibility, and is a possible forerunner of local salary negotiations which have been advocated quite widely.

The staffing issue is possibly more acute for primary schools. They have never enjoyed the benefits of curriculum-led staffing and it is unlikely that local authority formulae will take this into account. Therefore the myth will continue that good primary practitioners are adept at teaching all areas of the curriculum, supported by the notion that they are teachers of children first and subjects second. Implementation of school policies is also likely to prove harder in primary schools which have not experienced in recent years the concentration of purpose which public examinations bring about. Policies which have existed have therefore tended to be ignored by most teachers in primary schools. Even assuming a willingness to follow school policies in primary classrooms, the delivery of the curriculum is likely to be patchy given the shortage of omnicompetent teachers. Science teaching is a good example of an area which is likely to be neglected but which will be tested as a core subject in the National Curriculum. Widespread use of specialist teachers in primary schools may not be far away.

**Physical resources**

The planning of successful implementation should not be concerned just with the need to have competent teachers. The delivery of the curriculum also requires that their efforts are adequately resourced. Teaching materials commensurate with the work to be carried out are the most obvious need, particularly when direct comparisons may well be made by potential clients with other schools in the area. From a teacher's perspective it is crucial that resources are not just channelled into high profile equipment, such as computer suites or musical instruments, but are spread widely. National Curriculum guidance may strengthen the cases of 'cinderella' subject areas, such as religious education, which have never been well funded. Equally, teachers will be in a strong position to argue that the resource implications of policy statements have to be seen through within the finite resources available to the school.

Broader resourcing issues cannot be ignored either if implementation is to be carried out successfully. These have a wide range. At one level they would include teaching areas and allied facilities such as libraries and resources rooms or cupboards. Ancillary staff working either in the classroom or elsewhere in a support capacity also have a direct impact upon the quality of provision. Backup services which would need funding also extend to photocopiers, banda machines and telephones. Lastly, the in-service training of the classroom teachers should be considered under this heading, both in terms of teaching quality and of morale and motivation. Their travelling expenses could be at least as expensive as tuition fees and so have to be considered carefully.

## STAGE FOUR — BUDGETING

Once detailed plans exist for the teaching to be undertaken in the school the next step is to allocate money to these activities. Hence the budget provides the cutting edge of the preparatory stages already undertaken.

When the preparatory stages have been worked through, and once the amount of the budget is known, demand will always outstrip the financial supply. The imbalance will be lessened if the school is raising additional enterprise income, but **priorities** will probably have to be established. This can only be done with accurate information and so the quality of the implementation plans will be very important. All curriculum areas are likely to require a minimum level of financing below which the teaching will suffer. Additional money, however, should lead to measurable improvements, which can be evaluated later.

Such additional funds may come through several means. Imposition, consultation and participation are all managerial methods in common usage. The theory underpinning LMS, however, would suggest that teachers at the chalk face are best able to provide the information on which senior management teams or financial subcommittees should base their decisions. Given the imprecision with which budgets will be allocated in the early years of LMS, contingency funds will be needed. However, priority lists should be drawn up which would require greater expenditure than seems available at this stage. Thus, in the event of financial savings elsewhere, for example on staffing or heating bills, money can be vired (transferred) into established priority areas. Under LMS there is no virtue in underspending or in the maintenance of enormous contingency funds at the expense of an impoverished curriculum.

## STAGE FIVE — IMPLEMENTATION

The delivery of the curriculum remains in the hands of teaching staff. The quality of the implementation will depend in part on how the new realities of LMS are brought home to teachers and how they respond to the new situation. The interpersonal skills of managers in schools will be needed if the teaching is to proceed in the coherent manner suggested above and required by the new legislation. Hearts and minds will need to be won over even though these changes are based upon legislation. Greater involvement and participation are the most likely avenues to bring success since they allow the teachers to have some control over their new circumstances. However, teachers will look for benefits coming from LMS in the teaching in which they are primarily engaged. The onus will be on headteachers and governing bodies to ensure that this is brought about.

## STAGE SIX — EVALUATION

Teachers will be more accountable than ever before for their teaching. Indeed, external accountability must be matched by internal answerability in terms of the overall management plans of the school. Evaluation and appraisal will be cornerstones of these processes.

Job descriptions and school curriculum policies have given teachers greater role definition by which they can be held to account. Governing bodies will expect quantifiable outcomes to be presented which match their own policy requirements. They will look to the school's managers to provide such evidence. This evidence will also be used to indicate the quality of management in the school. As the managerial competence of governing bodies is increased it is to be expected that incompetent managers, like incompetent teachers, will be held to account.

# 8
# Management Action Points

We have concentrated in the previous chapter on the broad planning cycle a school will go through. What follows is a precise checklist of detailed activities that a school will have to undertake. Schools must address these key activities if they are to manage LMS successfully. It is a valuable exercise for a school to decide who does what (administrative staff or teaching staff or governors) and when during the school year.

**TASKS TO BE UNDERTAKEN DURING A SCHOOL YEAR**

**1. Decide the following broad policies & requirements:**
 (a) Curriculum and curriculum areas.
 (b) Numbers of teaching and non-teaching staff.
 (c) Needs of the building, eg repairs, decoration, health & safety.
 (d) Furniture and equipment needs.
 (e) Income raising, eg lettings, fund raising.
 (f) How much to keep for emergencies.

**2. Initial budgetary processes:**
 (a) Check amount of money given to the school by the LEA. Is it based on the correct pupil numbers?
 (b) Decide how much to allocate to each budgetary heading—staffing, maintenance etc.
 (c) Produce monthly forecast of spending—how much of the budget is spent by each month in the financial year.

**3. Place contracts for:**
 (a) Internal maintenance.
 (b) Later, after privatisation:
   (i) Cleaning.
   (ii) School meals.
   (iii) Grounds maintenance.

**4. Organise the administration and management of:**
   (a) Placing orders.
   (b) Invoices—check and send for payment.
   (c) Maintain school records.
   (d) Check LEA statements of expenditure.
   (e) Produce monthly monitoring statements.
   (f) Check whether expenditure is on target.
   (g) If needed, agree virement.

**5. Quality control mechanisms:**
Set up procedures to ensure that contracts have been fulfilled correctly. Is the new electrical wiring safe? Is the internal painting up to standard? Do you 'buy into' the LEA service for this?

**6. Reporting to parents:**
Set up the annual public meeting of parents including a financial report.

**7. Reporting to governors:**
Consider how you would set up effective reporting to/with governors:
   (a) How often?
   (b) What sequence, ie what time of the year?
   (c) Full governors' meeting or subcommittee?
   (d) Relationship with internal committee structure?

**8. Establish training plans:**
   (a) Organise briefing meeting for all staff to help them understand the nature and dimensions of the change. This is for teaching and non-teaching staff.
   (b) Governors to have similar introductory meeting.
   (c) Senior management team in a school to develop management skills and abilities in this field through training programme.
   (d) Governors, senior staff and LEA representatives to get together to assess how they are going to work together as a team to manage their new roles and responsibilities.
   (e) Training for administrative staff and senior management in the operation of administrative and management systems including the use of computer software programmes.
   (f) A useful description of training in practice is contained in Davies (1988) which looks at training in Leicestershire.

This chapter has provided schools with an action plan to put into immediate practice.

# 9
# Management Exercises and Case Studies

**EXERCISE 1: SECONDARY SCHOOL MANAGEMENT**

**Case Study A**
To help with the resource demands of GCSE, the Headteacher of a school wishes to create two additional support staffing posts: (a) resources technician, (b) an extra science technician. The Headteacher considers that the money for this could be found by reducing the teaching staff by one teacher.

Describe the strategy of the Head before taking this proposal to the Governors' Finance Committee.

**Case Study B**
*For Headmaster's intray, please*

Dear Mr Underspend,

As you know, last term we covered E. Retire's timetable within the department for a term, after his departure. We all worked a great deal extra. I gather from the registrar that the school saved £5,000 —but we have not seen any of it. Surely all the savings should come to our department.

C. Effective, Head of Economics.

Analyse what management issues arise in each case study and discuss with colleagues how to deal with them.

## EXERCISE 2: PRIMARY SCHOOL MANAGEMENT

### Case Study C

Mrs B. N. Around, the language coordinator, is to retire this term. The governors expect her to be replaced with another 'B' allowance teacher in order to maintain standards. However, the Head would rather appoint a probationer, who would be considerably cheaper, and a 0.4 ancillary to help in the office and some of the classes.

Describe the strategy of the Head before taking this proposal to the Governors' Finance Committee and outline the arguments s/he would use there.

### Case Study D

*For Head's intray, please*

Dear Mr Deficit,

As you know we have been having a concerted effort in the Infant Annex to cut down on our use of electricity for heating and lighting. As a result we have saved 2762 therms compared with last year's figure—which I recorded as you requested. At 8.6p a therm this means that we have saved £237.53. I think it would greatly encourage the children to continue with this if we could spend this on play apparatus for the infant playground. We have been through the catalogues and the equipment comes to £230. May we go ahead and order this?

Mrs C. Control, i/c Infant Annex.

Discuss how you would respond to this.

## EXERCISE 3: STAFFING CHOICE

Choosing between different types of staffing presents a major management task. The following represents the staffing costs of a secondary and a primary school:

|  | Primary School | Secondary School |
|---|---|---|
| Teaching Staff | £200,300 | £740,000 |
| Admin, Clerical & Classroom Support Staff | £ 16,600 | £ 41,000 |
| Caretakers & Cleaners | £ 12,500 | £ 50,000 |

## Management Exercises

The average annual cost of a teacher is £16,321 (including employer's superannuation etc) while the average cost of a clerical assistant is £7,500 (including employer's superannuation etc).

1. If the teachers in a secondary school give up one 'non-teaching' period and teach instead, a school with 38 staff could save one teaching post while one with 75 staff could save two teaching posts. What is the argument for doing this to buy more clerical assistance?
2. What problems do you see in implementing such a policy?
3. In a primary school what is the scope for choosing between extra part-time teaching staff or much cheaper primary assistants?

## EXERCISE 4: UNIT COSTS

**Hollybrook Primary**

| Expenditure | £'000 | £ per pupil N.O.R. 300* | £ per pupil N.O.R. 330 |
|---|---|---|---|
| Teachers | 198.5 | | |
| Support Staff | 12.9 | | |
| Premises Staff | 11.3 | | |
| Premises | | | |
|   Heat, Light | 13.5 | | |
|   Cleaning | | | |
|   Repairs | 3.9 | | |
|   Grounds | 0.6 | | |
|   Rent/Rates | 11.7 | | |
|   Other | 1.5 | | |
| | 253.9 | | |
| Books & Equipment | 5.6 | | |
| Other costs | 0.8 | | |
| *Net Expenditure* | 260.3 | | |

*N.O.R. = Number of Pupils on the School's Roll.

To establish the unit cost divide expenditure items by the number of children on roll.

1. Establish the unit costs for Hollybrook Primary School, based first on 300 children on roll (av. class size 27), and then on the figure of 330 children (av. class size 30).

2. What do these figures suggest might be the optimum N.O.R. for the school before it would be necessary to introduce extra staffing and/or teachers?

3. How would you argue against such an increase in class sizes if proposed by your Governing Body?

4. How would you attempt to sell the idea to your Governors if you were in favour of the idea?

## EXERCISE 5: UNIT COSTS

### St James' Secondary (N.O.R. 1150)

| Expenditure | £'000 | £ per pupil PTR 16.9 | £ per pupil PTR 17.9 |
|---|---|---|---|
| Teachers' Salaries 1 | | | |
| 2 | | | |

1. Calculate the teachers' salary bill in unit costs per pupil for St James' Comprehensive, using first 16.9 and then 17.9 as the PTR. Given staff reductions along these lines, how much would the school save—working on a figure of £16,321 as the average on-cost of a teacher?

2. If the 68 teachers at St James' were asked to give up one 'free' period a week for the year (40 period week), how much would the school save if the staffing base was cut accordingly?

3. If the existing staff was maintained, but the PTR was increased to 17.9 and the existing teachers reduced by one of their number of free periods, how much larger could the school grow prior to needing extra teaching staff?

*Note* PTR = Pupil/Teacher Ratio: the number of pupils divided by the number of teachers.

# EXERCISE 6

**Letting costs: Hollybrook Primary**

*Wages*

Caretaker £105 per week, plus £4.00 an hour overtime
Cleaner @ £2.89 per hour

| *Expenditure* | £'000 per annum |
|---|---|
| Premises | |
|   Heat, Light | 13.5 |
|   Cleaning | – |
|   Repairs | 3.9 |
|   Grounds | 0.6 |
|   Rent/Rates | 11.7 |
|   Other | 1.5 |

1. On the basis of these figures can you establish an hourly hiring charge for evening lettings of (a) one of the eleven classrooms; (b) the hall; (c) the building? What additional information might lead you to reach a more informed figure?

2. The Ramblers' Society would like to take over the school during the Christmas holiday for a week, so that it can be used as a base for a walking holiday for 40 of their members. What price per head would secure that the school did not lose financially on the venture? What profit margin would you seek?

3. The local Boys' Brigade would like to use your field one Saturday afternoon for an open air concert. How much would you charge? Would you increase the fee for a local Gymkhana, if so to what? How would you accurately estimate possible costs in either case?

# Appendix One

## THE SCHOOL BUDGET IN 1992 — WHAT A GOVERNORS' REPORT MIGHT LOOK LIKE

**Note**: How LMS will work out in the future is obviously difficult to predict. What is clear is that the nature of schools and school management will be very different. What follows is a speculative governors' report written by David Henderson, the head of a 6th form college predicting how a college within the new framework may run. This is done in a way which demonstrates what the future might hold for schools as attitudes and management approaches adapt to the new circumstances.

## 1991/92 FINANCIAL YEAR INTITIAL PLANNING DOCUMENT FOR THE ATTENTION OF THE COLLEGE GOVERNING BODY SUB-COMMITTEE MEETING TO BE HELD – NOVEMBER 1990

### 1. Background

Governors will recall that in the current financial year we have managed largely with historic cost levels for many of our budget headings and during the last 12 months the 8 meetings of the Finance Sub-Committee have been involved with a monitoring and learning role. Because of the continued growth of the College the effects of the formula-led budget have been offset by our ability to make savings on the teacher budget by effectively worsening our staffing ratio. Our curriculum planning strategies have also been heavily influenced by the increasing impact of the District TVEI thrust and the additional income that this has generated has meant that £8,500 has been made available for the development of new learning materials.

We have also been able to pioneer the development of Media

Technology courses. At this stage in the financial year, therefore, the Senior Management team are predicting that the budget out-turn figure for April 1991 will be within 1% of our cash limit figure.

## 2. County Policy 1991-92

From the information currently available it would appear that the County Council budget for the next financial year will be held at the present levels. With the advent of LMS the Director of Education has found it increasingly difficult to gain approval for growth items because there is no guarantee to the members that the money will necessarily find its way into the correct pocket. The complexities of the virement processes have meant that some members have been dismayed when cherished projects have been circumvented at local level. Our numbers appear to have peaked and the major trough predicted by the demographic down-turn suggests that our roll will fall next year by at least 5% and possibly as much as 8%. The range of the decline will be influenced by the degree of success that our new targeted marketing policy will produce (see paragraph 7).

## 3. Budget facts

Because of the features listed above it is estimated that the LEA formula for next year's budget will result in a reduction of an estimated 4%. In actual terms we believe that this will mean a reduction of approximately £52,000 on our current budget of £1,329,000. It is against this background that the governing body should look at the proposals for next year's cycle of spending in order to determine:

(a) Where savings can be made.
(b) Necessary trade-offs for the determination of priorities.

## 4. Overall development strategy

Senior Management of the college believe that it is crucial to maintain a forward planning strategy and suggest the following broad thrusts are maintained:

(a) Our policy of giving all students free entry to major course work examinations.
(b) Our intensive school marketing and advertising policy.
(c) The development of new 'A' and 'AS' levels in the current fashionable subjects of Design, Technology, Electronics and Media.

(d) The maintenance of traditional teaching styles in the accepted "academic" 'A' levels.
(e) The maintenance of our personal student counselling system.
(f) The continued development of Unit Accredited Courses which give clear progression and enhancement with the work that is going on 14-16 with the National Curriculum.

## 5. Staffing policies

The current teaching staff costs for the college are £1,127,000 in a full year (APT & C staff are an additional £65,000). The current budget for teachers includes £78,000 for incentive allowances. In terms of contracted posts we are currently running at principal + 2 vice-principals + 44 full-time teachers + 3 FTE + 1 post that is vired. As far as incentive allowances are concerned, through historic reasons, we have 70% of our staff with allowances, compared with the County funding level of 60%. We are particularly over-spending in our B band allowances with 5 teachers more than funded receiving the B allowance.

## 6. APT & C staff costs

The current points formula allocated to APT & C staff would give a budget of £56,000. The budget is currently running above this level because the governors decided last year that for Health and Safety reasons it was essential to appoint an additional Craft Technician. Over the last two years the amount of administration work taken on by APT & C staff has increased because of the much sharper focus on administrative activities within the college. This increase of work load has to some extent been offset by the continual development of high technology office equipment. The increased use of Apple Macintosh computers as personal productivity tools has shown great savings. However, the registrar now reports that the APT & C staff are currently working at 100% capability and in view of the difficulties that still exist in regrading there are serious problems in motivating staff whose average salary is less than £6,500 p.a. We have heard rumours that a local competing 11-18 school is considering offering APT & C staff additional bonus payments of up to £2,000 p.a. for a newly negotiated performance-linked structure.

## 7. Marketing

Over the last three years governors will have seen an increased level of marketing activities within all schools in the district. As the 16-19 population dwindles we must continue to work hard to maintain our share of the market. Our techniques have become more sophisticated as time has passed and in particular I am very pleased with the way in which our targeted approach seems to be working. The fact that our computer databases now hold details of the last 14 years' student population gives us very close information on our selective mail shots to those youngsters who have had either friends or relations within the college. The new short duration promotional videos which are sent out on free loan, coupled with our Wine and Cheese evenings are resulting in continuing leadership in this field. The overall marketing budget for last year was £8,500 of which £4,500 was staff time. Our intelligence unit has discovered that other local 11-18 schools are able to spend far more than this and at least two of them are using the considerable funds that they can raise from lower school parents events to generate marketing budgets in excess of £10,000 p.a.

## 8. Curriculum costs

Last year's Curriculum Planning Group obtained governors' permission to spend the following amounts of money resourcing our various programmes:

| | |
|---|---|
| Science/Technology Faculty | £8,500 |
| Creative Arts Faculty | £5,400 |
| Humanities Faculty | £6,200 |
| Pre-vocational Faculty | £2,200 |

In essence these figures were determined from previous historic costs elements. However, during the last year the Curriculum Planning Group has been looking at quantifiable outcomes and measurable performance indicators. Some interesting figures emerge for Faculty spending if success at 'A' level is taken as a quantifiable performance indicator. The following figures illustrate this point:

| Subject | Resources alloc. over 2 years | Number of 'A' level passes in year | Teacher cost | Cost per student |
|---|---|---|---|---|
| Maths | £   650 | 47 | £9,900 | £224 |
| Design | £1,450 | 6 | £3,300 | £791 |
| Physics | £1,500 | 38 | £6,600 | £213 |

The basis for the above calculations is to assume a cost of £11/hr, 5 hours/week, for approximately 60 weeks over the two years. Clearly the above figures give only a general guide and a group of senior management are working on a computer programme which will give far more accurate costs taking into account such variables as room size, energy utilisation, student dropout rate, and utilisation of centrally funded resources such as library, technicians, videos etc.

However, even from preliminary work it is clear that the county's policy of non-weighted formula funding leads to some tremendous anomalies in subject costs. Certainly our worst examples are those 'A' levels which are taught in small groups and require high levels of technical support and material utilisation.

## 9. Income generation

Over the last few years our main source of supplementary income has been the work we do with YTS off-the-job training. Fees per annum for this work average around £12-14,000 and by judicious use of infill classes it is calculated that approximately 50% of this income is clear profit. The potential for additional work in this area is declining as more managing agents do their own in-house training and as FE colleges become more and more competitive. Additional income generation is being considered along with sponsorship. Unfortunately the College does not possess a large sports/leisure complex, as found in other institutions, but we need to give consideration to running our own adult classes. Initial marketing research in this area would show that our more advanced facilities for Design, Photography, Computing and Business Studies, as well as the usefulness of our hall and larger spaces for other meetings, could generate considerable income. Sponsorship could be made much more positive and it is suggested that consideration should be given to the appointment of a **Sponsorship Manager** working to a commission equal to 10% of revenue generated. A telephone and office accommodation could be made available by modifications to existing rooms and it is felt that sufficient candidates of good calibre would come forward from those people who have taken early retirement having had a marketing, PR or financial background.

## 10. Premises

I am pleased to report that the overall condition of the premises is good and the continuous programme of development over the last five years has meant that there are no over-riding problems at the moment. However, the new requirements to pay for our own maintenance have meant that we have gone over budget in the last two years on reglazing damaged windows. We are unfortunate that many of our new windows are tinted glass double-glazed fitments which are extremely expensive to repair and, in the case of 25 of them, located in a particularly hazardous position in the Design Centre where hydraulic lifting apparatus must be used to enable workmen to reach them. The average cost of repairing one of these windows is 1000% greater than the formula figure determines. It is estimated that unless we take action the repair bill next year could exceed £5,000. The question of general site security following last year's break-in, which resulted in damage and loss of equipment to the value of £26,000, means that there is some urgency in considering whether we should employ our own security patrol and to what extent we should renegotiate our Building Insurance policies. Preliminary discussions with a local firm of highly regarded solicitors would indicate that they would be prepared to offer a total package of legal and insurance advice at what appears to be an extremely competitive figure compared with current county rates. The ability to have instant communication with experienced legal advice would be reassuring to the senior staff here.

## 11. Competitive tendering

The first set of contracts that were signed in 1989/90 are now coming up for review and initial reports indicate that whilst we are more than satisfied with grounds maintenance and cleaning contracts, we are much less satisfied with catering. I have now been approached by two colleagues who have indicated that we should give consideration to taking over the whole of the catering within the college, setting up a separate limited company. They have produced an initial business plan concentrating on a fast-food serv-ice and utilising large amounts of part-time student labour. This is a particularly attractive part of the scheme in that it would mean that some of our students who have considerable financial difficulties would get access to new part-time jobs on site. It is suggested that a governors' sub-committee called the Catering Development Unit should look at the whole possibility of forming our own private company, aiming to produce a business plan suitable for generating an advance loan from our bankers.

## 12. Teacher staff merit payments/performance linked
Governors need to be made aware that a number of schools in the North West and elsewhere are tentatively looking at performance linked bonuses for school and college staff. These are applied right across the provision and I know of at least two schools where the headteachers can obtain an annual performance bonus of up to £5,000 for reaching certain criteria specified by the Governors. It is suggested that a sum of between £10,000/£15,000 could be allocated on an experimental basis during the next year or so for either increased performance or extra hours in the classroom.

## 13. The way ahead
Final decisions regarding the College budget need to be approved in detail at the full Governors' Meeting next February. In the meantime Sub-Committee meetings need to be held to discuss the way ahead from the report produced herewith. If it is decided that there needs to be a reduction in staff levels then it will need to be borne in mind that simply removing part-time teachers will not work because some of our key minority subjects are taught in this way. The confidential Part 2 of this report lists certain members of staff whose services we could perhaps do without, particularly if the core staff remaining were involved with some form of bonus payment. Whether it would be possible to remove teachers' incentive allowances is problematical and I believe that there is currently a test case going through the courts on this very issue. Likewise, the recent 3 industrial tribunal findings at which schools and LEAs were taken to task for ineptly handling redundancy and dismissal, with damages in excess of £50,000 per teacher, would indicate the need for some sensitivity and perhaps prudence in this matter.

*Your obedient servant*
*David Henderson*
*Principal*

# Appendix 2

## OBTAINING GRANT MAINTAINED STATUS (GMS) — OPTING OUT

While this book concentrates on delegated school finance and is not about opting out, the authors consider that the issues are related. Some schools will be evaluating the financial implications of opting out as well as those of delegated budgets. Opting out of LEA control means that the school becomes funded directly by the Department of Education and Science and is responsible for all its expenditure including those areas previously retained by the LEA. The school which lacks enough pupils to generate a sufficient budget will not receive any extra money for those pupils as such. What it will receive is its share of the money that the LEA retained for central administration, etc, as outlined in Chapter One. The financial considerations that a school will have to review are listed below. These were first published by Davies (1989) in *Education* (10.02.89) and are reproduced by kind permission of Longman Ltd.

### "No school with a flat roof can ever opt out"

Some schools are assessing the financial and other factors that underlie the decision to opt out of Local Authority control. An examination of some schools potentially in this category suggests that their motivation is not an economic one, but based on other factors. The threat to a selective intake, falling pupil numbers or the removal of 6th form pupils to rationalise local provision are common reasons that have come to the surface. It is interesting to speculate how ministers will resolve the conflict between long-held policies of reducing excess capacity in parts of the secondary sector and the fact that LEAs' attempts to do that will prompt threatened schools to opt out. Supporting 'opting out' could mean supporting uneconomic schools under a different guise.

Schools thinking of opting out will obviously be doing some careful calculations over the next few years as details of LEA costs, and the amount of equivalent central funding which the DES will provide, become known. What follows is a strategic view of some of the key issues. It will provide school decision-makers with a checklist against which to assess the economic viability of opting out.

**Pupil roll and characteristics plus future projections**
In a system to be financed on a pupil-number-driven formula for 75% of a school's income, the number of pupils is clearly a critical factor. The existing number of pupils will determine the immediate budget. However, two key factors for the future are the characteristics of those pupils and future projections of intake. If the school is a secondary one with a 6th form then the type of pupil and how well he is treated and educated will determine staying on rates between the 5th and 6th forms. In both the primary and secondary sectors the future intake is determined by the total number of pupils in an area and the share which that particular school is able to attract. Marketing will obviously be a key factor. On current education management courses LMS, marketing and stress are the subjects in greatest demand. Is there a correlation? Building up a 3 to 5 year projection will be essential if schools are to provide themselves with a budget that can be viable not only immediately but also over the medium term. This is the first key factor that a school must assess in considering grant maintained status.

**Existing condition of property and plant**
The Government stresses its 'level playing field' philosophy, in that all schools will be treated equitably by a clearly understood financial distribution formula. In the literal sense some schools do not have playing fields at all and others have verdant acres; but the inequality of existing provision goes much further than this. Some schools have had significant rebuilding, repair and maintenance in recent years and will be in a much stronger position than other schools. They will not have to spend so much on these items. The initial quotation about 'flat roofs' means that some schools with flat roofs will have significant future maintenance costs while others will not. This second factor is critical. Costs may seem fundable now, but long term maintenance costs may cripple the future viability of grant maintained schools.

### Age profile of the staff

A third factor in assessing the economic viability of opting out is not just the number of teachers employed but also their age profile. The Audit Commission Report (1988) compared schools with younger average age staff on lower scales with similar schools with older staff on higher scales. Since this Report the significance of staffing costs has been increasingly recognised. Most LEAs have run costing data through their computers which show disparities between actual and average costs in their schools. In the secondary sector this can produce anything between a £30,000 deficit and a £45,000 surplus. Thus, it will either prove a major burden or a windfall for a school. Knowing exact costs in the staffing field and the effects of 'incremental drift' will be key factors.

### Whether the school was above or below average costs for the LEA

Putting these first three factors together provides a fourth overall guide. Unit costs comparisons already show wide variations in the average cost per pupil both in the primary and secondary sectors. These will either work to the advantage or detriment of schools as formula funding has its effect. Thus a school needs to find out how its individual unit costs compare with the LEA average. This, in the short term, is the most critical individual factor determining the economic viability of opting out.

### Other external funding

A fifth economic factor may be the extent of non-government funding. Sponsorship, parental voluntary contributions through PTAs and covenant schemes may provide critical revenue. Some schools have favourable catchment areas and community links to raise extra funds; others contrast sharply.

### The school's view of the quality of LEA service — could it obtain better externally?

If a school thinks it gets good service from the LEA departments there will be little incentive to go through the upheaval of opting out. However, if LEA departments do not realise that they are in a market situation in supplying the schools then the schools, if dissatisfied, may take their custom elsewhere. If they can also get this service more cheaply, the pressure to opt out may be hard to resist. This sixth factor is one that is of equal importance to schools and to LEAs who want to keep them.

**Incentives for opting out**
Government policy now is to treat opted out and remaining LEA schools in the same way. But will this change? City Technology Colleges prove that the Government operates differential resourcing. Will this come to cover opted out schools as well? A main consideration then will be whether the funding regime will stay the same or whether it will change. This final factor is difficult to assess as policy changes by politicians are not unknown.

**Conclusion**
These seven key economic factors provide the critical resource issues for schools to consider as they struggle with the opting out dilemma. However, a word about LEAs. While we suggested that no school with a flat roof could opt out because of the future maintenance costs, maybe the LEAs want all their schools with flat roofs to opt out!

# Glossary

**Academic year.** This runs from September until August.

**Advisory teachers** have areas of curriculum expertise and knowledge which they use to train and develop other teachers in schools.

**Ancillary helpers** are classroom assistants who are often attached to children with learning difficulties or help out in infant classrooms.

**Capital expenditure** refers to money set aside for major new building or other long term programmes.

**Capitation** is the term given to the budgets that schools have received in the past, based on pupils' age and numbers, from which they have bought books and educational equipment.

**Competitive tendering.** Under this system a number of firms or companies are asked to put in bids for work to be done. The school can choose the quote best suited to its budget and requirements.

**Contingency fund.** A sum of money put to one side for unforeseen or unquantifiable future expenditure.

**Coopers and Lybrand Report.** Commissioned from the leading firm of chartered accountants by the DES, and subsequently influential in setting the direction in which LMS would go.

**Financial year.** This runs from April 1st until March 31st.

**'Floating' teachers** have no particular class teacher role, but support the curriculum throughout the primary schools where they work in a number of different ways.

**Formula.** The means by which LEAs will share out the money available for delegated school budgets.

**Historical budgeting** is the practice of basing one year's budget on what had been received the year before.

**Incentive allowances** are usually paid to teachers who take on additional responsibilities, such as curriculum leadership roles, in schools.

**Incremental budgets** are associated with historical costings and are the annual adjustments made to the figures to allow for minor adjustments but the budget remains the same.

**Incremental scales.** These are the rungs of the pay ladder that teachers climb on an annual basis up to a maximum point.

**Open enrolment** is where parents can choose between schools for their children's education.

**Peripatetic teachers** travel from school to school teaching specialist subjects such as music.

**Special units** are classes created for children with severe learning problems.

**Statemented children** are those who have been referred to the LEA's educational psychologists who have considered the child's prob-lems serious enough to merit their being kept under annual review. These reports are the child's statements.

**Supply teachers** are extra staff brought in to cover for sick or absent teachers.

**Virement.** The transfer of money from one expenditure heading to another.

**Voucher scheme.** This is where parents are given the cash 'vouchers' which they pass on to the school which they have chosen for their children's education. This would apply to all types of school, and both private and local authority schools.

# Further Reading

1. Audit Commission, *Obtaining Better Value in Education* (1984).
2. Audit Commission, *Towards Better Management of Secondary Education* (1986).
3. Audit Commission, *Delegation of Management Authority to Schools* (1988). Occasional Paper No 5.
4. Caldwell, B.J. with Spinks, J.M., *The Self-Managing School*, (Falmer Press 1988).
5. Coopers & Lybrand Associates, *Local Management of Schools: A Report to the Department of Education and Science* (HMSO 1988).
6. Davies, K.B., 'The Key Issues of Financial Delegation', *Education* Vol 170 No 18 (30th October 1987).
7. Davies, K.B., 'Three Steps to Lift-Off: Unfolding an LFM Training Strategy in Leicestershire', *Education* Vol 172 No 6 (5th August 1988).
8. Davies, K.B., 'School Capitation and its Distribution: Is the Weight of Opinion Changing?', with Ellison, L., *School Organisation* Vol 7 No 1 (1987). Part reproduced in OU course E325.
9. Downes, P., *Local Financial Management in Schools* (Blackwell 1988).
10. Knight, B., *Managing School Finance* (Heinemann 1983).
11. Thomas, H., 'Pupils as Vouchers', *Times Educational Supplement* (2nd December 1988).
12. Thomas, H., *Local Management of Schools in Action* (Cassell 1989).

# Useful Addresses

Assistant Masters and Mistresses Association, 7 Northumberland Street, London WC2N 5DA.

Audit Commission, 157-197 Buckingham Palace Road, London SW1W 9SP.

Campaign for the Advancement of State Education, President Joan Sallis, 49 Lauderdale Drive, Petersham, Richmond, Surrey.

Chartered Institute of Public Finance and Accountancy, 3 Robert Street, London WC2N 6BH.

Centre for the Study of Comprehensive Schools, Wentworth College, University of York, York YO1 5DD.

Department of Education and Science, Elizabeth House, York Road, London SE1 7PH.

Industrial Society, Peter Runge House, 3 Carlton House Terrace, London SW1Y 5DG.

National Association of Head Teachers, Holly House, 6 Paddockhall Rd, Haywards Heath, West Sussex RH16 1RG.

National Association of Governors and Managers, 81 Rustlings Road, Sheffield S11 7AB.

National Association of School Masters/Union of Women Teachers, Hillscourt Education Centre, Rose Hill, Rednal, Birmingham B45 8RS.

National Confederation of Parent Teacher Associations, 43 Stonebridge Road, Northfleet, Gravesend, Kent DA11 9DS.

National Union of Teachers, Hamilton House, Mabledon Place, London WC1H 9BD.

Society of Education Officers, 21-27 Lambs Conduit St, London WC1N 3NJ.

Secondary Headteachers Association, Chancery House, 107 St Paul's Road, London N1 2NB.

# Index

Allowances, incentive, 41
Budgets, aggregated, 13
   delegated, 14
   general, 13, 15
   historical, 15, 22, 92
   incremental, 16, 23, 92
   skills for, 25
Cambridgeshire, 36
   pilot scheme, 22
Competitive tendering, 18, 85, 91
Coopers & Lybrand Report, 24-25, 91
Cost centres, 11
Costs, employee, 15-17, 32, 39-43
   non-teaching staff, 42, 43, 82
   premises-related, 15, 43-44, 84-85
   services, 32, 44-45
   schools' fixed, 29-30
   schools' variable, 29-30
   teaching staff, 15-17, 32, 39-43
Delegated finance, 8, 11, 13
   government's objectives, 11-12
   pilot schemes, 15-16, 22-28
   scope of, 12
Department of Education & Science Circular 7/1988, 26, 43
Devolved finance, 11
Education, market model, 20
Education Reform Act, 17, 39, 47
Employee costs, 15-17, 39-43
Employers and LMS, 65-66
Expenses, contingency, 46, 91
   establishment, 32, 45
   miscellaneous, 32, 45-46

Formula funding, 16, 18, 22-24, 39, 92
Governors, accountability of, 60
   and budgets, 59-60
   curriculum, 57-58
   insurance, 15
   management plans, 56-60
   new responsibilities, 12, 26, 55-60
   staffing, 17, 58-59
   training schemes, 18
Grant Maintained Status, 87-90
Grants, education support, 14
   EEC, 14
   Section Eleven, 14
   Travellers' children's, 14
   TVEI, 14
Headteachers, 47-54, 67-72
Health and safety legislation, 43
Income generation, 32, 50-54, 84
Incentive allowances, 41
Information technology, 36
Inner London Education Authority (ILEA) AUR pilot scheme, 22
Insurance, governors, 15
   schools, 15, 45
Local Education Authorities (LEAs) budget allocations, 13-15
   contingency reserves, 15
   discretionary exceptions, 14-15
   formula funding, 16, 18, 22-24, 39
   **grant support system, 7-8**

# Index

monitoring of performance, 62-63
pilot schemes, 22-28
strategic role of, 25-26, 60-62
training schemes, 18
Local financial management, 11
Local Government Act 1988, 18, 44
Local management of schools, 11-21
implementation of, 18
outline of, 8
Marketing, 49-50, 82-83
Management, action points, 73-74
information systems, 18, 25, 33-36
plans, 9, 24, 40, 67-72
Open enrolment, 8, 47-49, 64-65, 92
Parents and LMS, 64
Participation, 24, 38, 71
Performance indicators, 20
Planning cycle, 19, 67-72
Premises-related costs, 32, 43-44
Pupils and LMS, 64-65
statemented, 15, 92

School, accountability of, 8-9, 60, 71-72
budgets, 11, 31-46
costs, 29-32
insurance, 15, 45
management action points, 73-74
marketing of, 49-50
sponsorship of, 53-54
supplies and services, 32, 44-45
Secretary of State for Education, 14
Solihull pilot scheme, 22-23, 27
Special schools, 12, 92
Sponsorship, 53-54
Staffing, costs, 15-17, 32, 39-43
governors' powers, 17, 39-43
non-teacher, 42-43, 82
Teachers, advisory, 15, 45, 91
and LMS, 63-64, 86
peripatetic, 15, 45, 92
supply, 42
Training schemes, governors, 18
teachers, 27
Virement, 36-37, 92